THE AMERICAN DREAM
UNREALIZED

Robert J. Krakower

ON TASK PUBLISHING

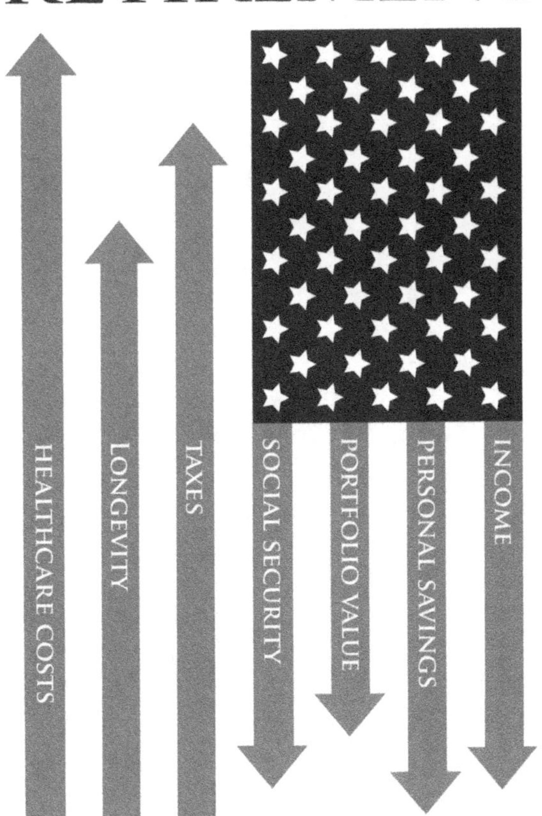
THE AMERICAN DREAM
UNREALIZED
YOUR LAST CHANCE TO RECLAIM YOUR
RETIREMENT
HEALTHCARE COSTS
LONGEVITY
TAXES
SOCIAL SECURITY
PORTFOLIO VALUE
PERSONAL SAVINGS
INCOME

CONTENTS

I dedicate this book to

Lori, Samantha, and Nicholas

"Life is a journey not a destination"

I am proud to have you on my journey through life

FOREWORD

When you see a funnel cloud on the horizon, you know a tornado is coming. You have two choices: hope it bypasses and doesn't whirl you and your family into the air, or take shelter in the storm cellar you built for just such an eventuality.

Similarly, people approaching retirement face an impending financial storm. Nearly 80 million Baby Boomers have or are about to retire. They are living longer than any previous generation and overwhelming the Social Security safety net. Government data indicates only a small percentage have saved enough to assure they don't run out of money before they die. The Social Security system that was supposed to provide for their retirement is threatened with insolvency. A financial tornado is approaching and most people facing retirement are frightfully unprepared.

Most people seem to recognize that Social Security will not provide what they need for a secure retirement, if it is available at all once they reach retirement age. Despite this acknowledgment, most lack a plan for generating sufficient retirement income. These people represent the Hidden Generation, the tail end of the Baby Boomers who will find it difficult to find a storm cellar refuge once that financial tornado appears.

Investors have never had access to more knowledge about money and investing yet been more confused about how best to save for retirement. With the dramatic shift from guaranteed defined benefit pension plans to defined contribution 401(k) plans, individuals are now responsible for their own retirement benefits. By default, they have become their own financial advisors. It appears precious few are prepared for the responsibility.

You can't rely on the advice of the media or well-intentioned friends or relatives to solve the problem for you. And you darn sure can't rely on the political class in Washington to come up with a solution.

The message is clear: if you hope to experience the American dream in retirement, you had better figure it out for yourself.

You need consistent, reliable income if you are to maintain the same standard of living in retirement that you enjoyed during your working years. You have to shift your thinking. Retirement planning now means portfolio growth must take a back seat to income. If you understand that you are responsible for your own safe retirement, you better be a forward thinker. As author Robert J. Krakower notes:

> *We know what to do but we don't do what we know.*
>
> *We've never been more educated and yet more confused.*
>
> *We've never had more resources and done less with them.*
>
> *We've never had more reasons to succeed and yet wasted more time.*

In this book—his second on the topic—Krakower opens the readers' eyes to the need to redefine their retirement. He guides you to strategies to help meet the challenges of financing your retirement without abandoning your lifestyle or forgoing the realistic pleasures you envision for the future. It can be done, but only if you will take personal responsibility for your retirement and explore the available investment alternatives.

— XI —

Michael Dubes
Front Page Media

INTRODUCTION

While gathering notes for my first book back in 2006, I was asked to speak on a panel discussing retirement issues. While waiting my turn, I heard another panelist talking about reverse mortgages. I was not familiar with the strategy at the time and so listened closely to what he had to say...and what he revealed startled me. He was warning about the alarming number of seniors compromising their security by selling off the equity in their homes in order to survive financially.

That was a seminal moment for me. As a successful financial advisor, I was doing fine, but when the enormity of this problem struck me I thought, "This is the American dream unrealized."

For as long as I can recall, we have been sold the fictional idea of the American dream for retirement: sailing off into the sunset of our golden years. Advertisements reinforce the image. Everything will be fine if you invest your money with us or buy our mutual fund.

Seniors sacrificing their home equity so they can eat and pay their utility bills was not part of the fantasy. The lack of financial strategies available to provide replacement income for seniors is discouraging and our industry has done little to address the issue. There's really no incentive for the industry—or our government leaders—to tackle this serious problem.

The hackneyed maxim of growing your assets through a buy and hold strategy no longer applies to individuals in or near retirement. Shorter market cycles and increased volatility mean portfolios now face a potential twenty or thirty percent drop in value every four or five years. Decades ago, retirees might experience one of these big drops; today, seniors might experience a half dozen or more market eruptions during their retirement.

The culprit is longevity. Modern medicine's endless quest to prolong life has produced a double-edged sword. We are living longer then ever and it's creating enormous pressure on government and the business community. The concept of retirement's three legged stool (pensions, Social Security and personal savings) is being challenged by the reality that people may now have a retirement as long as their working years.

In my first book, *Redefining Retirement for a New Generation*, I outlined how the confluence of several factors—longevity, the shift from company pensions to 401(k) plans and the diminished role of Social Security— had created the first true crisis in the history of the U.S. retirement system. Throw in the bottleneck being created by 79 million retiring Baby Boomers and you have an impending retirement crisis of epic proportions.

In the years that have passed since 2006 when I wrote my book, nothing has happened to change that equation. At the time, the credit meltdown of 2009 was not yet on anyone's radar but I foresaw the need to find alternatives to diversify the way investors viewed total return.

Once the bubble burst, another bubble was born, created by the Fed artificially depressing interest rates so as to keep a staggering economy inching along. What this artificial engineering seems to have wrought is an accelerated boom-bust cycle. Whether an aberration or the new economic normality, we may have painted ourselves into a corner from which extrication will be difficult if not impossible.

How do we plan for a secure retirement in this shifting paradigm?

In addition to shorter boom-bust cycles, what happens when the full impact of the avalanche of retiring Baby Boomers is felt? What happens when the number of retirees is double the number of workers actively contributing to Social Security? As of today, we still have a functioning Social Security system. What will happen to the generation that follows the Baby Boomers when Social Security plays a significantly reduced role in their retirement income? What happens when there are no more retirees receiving guaranteed benefits from their company pensions? What happens when our historically low savings rate converges with our historically low birth rate?

The challenge for tomorrow's retirees will be how to maintain a decent standard of living for 30 or 40 years without two legs of the proverbial stool—pensions and Social Security—and facing a recurring bubble of market downturns?

Look around and ask yourself who is going to help solve the problem. Do you see our leaders coming together to offer realistic solutions? We've become a nation that doesn't want to deal with its problems. Nothing gets solved. Politicians, business leaders and the media will, no doubt, continue to expound on the need to do something but nothing of consequence will be accomplished on a grand scale. To the contrary, government is easing its way out of the retirement business at all levels and abdicating responsibility to the individual.

The message is clear: if you hope to experience the American dream in retirement, you had better figure it out for yourself.

The onus for providing retirement income has been passed on from company pensions to individual 401(k) accounts. The greatest transfer of risk in the history of this country has taken place and you are being sold the illusion that it is good for you because you are now actively participating in the outcome.

Despite having shifted all the financial risk associated with providing retirement income over to you, there's no roadmap to point you in the right direction towards a secure retirement. There's no risk-free method of saving for an extended retirement. You can no longer rely on bank deposits or similar fixed-income investments to generate adequate retirement income because the rate of return doesn't even keep pace with inflation. Instead, you may be inexorably funneled into risky investments in an increasingly volatile market environment.

My goal in writing this book is not to frighten you but rather to make you aware of the impending crisis while introducing you to the options available to help counteract its impact. If you have a medical issue, you seek out a treatment or cure. Right now, no one has created a medication to cure the retirement crisis. Its full effect has not yet been felt but virtually everyone recognizes it's on the horizon. It's your future and it will get here quickly.

There are a few who are not content to wait and see if someone will fix this problem; those who will assume personal responsibility and create their own self-security to replace what will no longer be there when they retire. I want you to be one of those people. I don't want you to become a passive victim, believing things are beyond your control.

I'm in the same boat as you. Now in my fifties, I will likely be close to age 70 before I can begin receiving Social Security, assuming it will still be there. When I do, it's not going to be comparable to the amount past generations received and were able to live on.

I'm a successful financial advisor and I'm frustrated with the system. I want to be proud of the job I'm doing to help my clients but the forces working against me are powerful. We're ambling down a road to retirement that's under construction and it's highly questionable whether we will reach our destination. The rubble that was once the American dream lies all around us. Yet we remain on that treacherous path, hoping for the best but not knowing where it will take us. In this book, I suggest we pull over and think about whether there is a way around these problems.

The financial industry is unlikely to change. There's little reason to do so because the status quo is highly profitable. I may not have all the answers but I'm engaged in the process and willing to explore how we as advisors can do better to help our clients generate replacement income for retirement.

We have to begin thinking outside the box. In this book, I'm going to travel the road to retirement with you, assess the problems you face and help you find an alternative to becoming a victim. I want to help you feel more confident about arriving at your destination with the ability to enjoy it. We both know the obstacles that stand in your way. You can ignore them and hope to be saved by external forces or you can take action and save yourself. I hope to help you start the process.

CHAPTER ONE

OUR DISCONNECTED SOCIETY

We know what to do but we don't do what we know.

We've never been more educated and yet more confused.

We've never had more resources and done less with them.

We've never had more reasons to succeed and yet wasted more time.

These words could apply to almost anything in today's world: economics, politics, education, social issues, religion, international disputes, and even physical fitness. It most certainly applies to planning and investing for retirement.

I am often asked to speak or make presentations to investors. Invariably, they tell me they are increasingly convinced that while taxes will rise, government retirement benefits will decline. They want to be optimistic that the same government will somehow find a solution and salvage their benefits but it's hard for them to find a reason for confidence. They are seeking an alternative solution, one that provides the psychological reassurance that they will be able to retire and maintain their lifestyle. Simply put, they hope to live the kind of retirement every American dreams of.

Given they are living longer and will have less Social Security benefits, the irrefutable fact is they must take greater personal responsibility for their financial future. Sadly, many do not.

Investors have never had access to more knowledge about money and investing yet been more confused about how best to save for retirement. Confusion often leads to apathy, the feeling that "there's nothing I can do about it." Once investors become apathetic, they typically stop thinking about the problem because they see no solution.

According to Ohio State University's thelantern.com, "Apathy is becoming an American plague. Most citizens today are worried less about the state of our union and more about the entertainment options at our disposal. Instead of becoming more proactive, many Americans have chosen to play hot potato with their responsibilities, thinking someone else will swoop in to save the day and solve their problems."

That assessment may be a bit harsh, but it illustrates the need for Americans to take the problem seriously and search for solutions. Those who fail to do so face the very real prospect of a retirement with few palatable options.

As a nation, America faces the possibility of declining like the Roman Empire in its latter days, where citizens became richer, lazier and unhappier than ever. In his 1975 essay, Edward Goldsmith writes, "It is said of the Bourbons that during the time they were in power, they neither learned nor forgot anything. This could equally well be said of our political leaders, probably too, of the scientists and economists who advise them. It is a great tragedy that we seem incapable of learning the lessons of history."

The lethargy that plagues today's society produces a dangerous collective mindset: the belief that problems will somehow work themselves out if we wait long enough. This misconception is an especially hazardous conviction for investors approaching retirement.

REALITY LOOMS

The 70 million Baby Boomers approaching or already in retirement cannot afford to ignore the confluence of obstacles facing them. On average, they are living longer than ever and will need more money in retirement than any previous generation. But two previously dependable sources of retirement income are now endangered and facing extinction. Social Security threatens to become unsustainable as the number of workers who contribute dwindles while the number receiving benefits soars. In addition, fewer retirees can now rely on guaranteed benefits because of the shift from corporate defined benefit plans to 401(k) plans managed by individuals.

While a disinterested society is otherwise engaged on Facebook, cell phone texting or playing fantasy football, those saving for retirement cannot be indifferent to these issues. They must acknowledge the problem, open a serious dialogue and find workable solutions.

Who will lift the country out of its apathetic malaise?

Certainly not our political leaders, who have forgotten how to lead. Today's politicians, like most of those who came before them, simply kick the can down the road when it comes to finding solutions. Every recent generation has done the same so the problems perpetuate indefinitely and grow worse. And it's sad because today we have the resources and education to know what to do and all the reasons to succeed. What we lack is the wisdom and vigor to do it.

The media plays a significant role in this self-fulfilling prophecy by helping perpetuate our disconnected society. It's in their interest to do so, of course, because the noise they create with self-serving propaganda distracts investors from the realities surrounding retirement. Financial news shows and their Wall Street advertisers create a fantasy world, where viewers are assured that all their retirement worries can be resolved by investing with this brokerage firm or that insurance company.

When it comes to your money, you must learn to tune out the noise generated by the media, the politicians and others. None of what they are promoting will help you reach your financial goals or secure a fulfilling retirement. The responsibility for achieving the American dream is yours.

> *The trouble with this world is apathy; but then who cares?"*

—LUCY FROM THE COMIC STRIP PEANUTS

YOUR PERSONAL CHALLENGE

We've never been more educated and yet more confused.

How best to invest for retirement in this environment? As mentioned, a large chunk of financial responsibility has been turned over to individuals via the 401(k). By default, they have become their own financial advisors and benefactors. How many are adequately prepared to manage their retirement portfolio? If the investors I talk to at financial seminars are any indication, precious few. The financial markets are increasingly more volatile and complex. It is an arena fraught with danger, yet novice investors are sent into battle without armor or adequate weaponry. They wander into the arena, hoping to survive on instinct or blind luck. That's not a reliable battle plan.

"If you start drinking, smoking and eating fatty food, you'll have enough retirement money to last the rest of your life."

What's the landscape of this battlefield? We are immersed in the time of the greatest transfer of risk in the history of our country and few investors recognize what is happening. You are told that you are now in charge of your own future, that managing your own 401(k) can produce a better financial result than having a guaranteed pension benefit from your employer. You're told that you are now going to participate in the outcome of the market, as if a successful outcome is assured.

It is not. It's a monolithic market. It is volatile and large movements up and down are commonplace. You are thrust into this arena and responsible for managing the chaos. The money you rely on to carry you to and through decades of retirement is at stake. As a small investor, it's difficult for you to participate at the level of the major market makers. Despite all you hear from the talking heads on the financial networks and the companies who pump out an endless array of alluring financial products, you are ultimately accountable for what happens to your money. This is no time to be disconnected or blithely hopeful.

Whereas you could previously rely on guaranteed income from Social Security and pensions in addition to your private savings, the latter is now the most important—and probably the only reliable—part of that triumvirate. In the past, if you lost your personal savings, you still had the other two checks coming in each month. That's no longer the case. The road to retirement now has a treacherous dropoff!

You are told your 401(k) puts you in control of your retirement but you have not been given the tools needed to do a competent job. Here's what stands in your way:

- You are restricted to investing in the mutual funds allowed by the custodian of your 401(k).

- If your financial advisor does not have a relationship with the funds, he may be cut out of the loop.

- Alternative products to help you achieve success in managing your retirement may be excluded from your 401(k).

- Your 401(k) may have hidden fees.

Many people I talk to believe their 401(k) is free. They don't realize that the undisclosed fees may make it more expensive than many other investments. The much-touted tax break you get on the front end may be minimal compared to the taxes due when you withdraw your money. The common misconception is that you will pay less in taxes during retirement but while you may have a lower marginal tax rate, you may have a higher effective rate because you will no longer have many deductions. And you are required to begin taking minimum withdrawals from your 401(k) at age 70.5. Failure to do so triggers a 50% levy courtesy of the IRS.

What are your choices? If you put your retirement funds in the bank or a CD, you may find it difficult to live on their returns, especially during an historically low interest rate environment such as we are presently experiencing. You are forced to plunge into a congested financial freeway, hoping to somehow avoid the road hazards, detours and dropoffs created by a volatile market and the financial industry. Those who do not adhere to the rules of the road will test your knowledge and driving skills. They can be dangerous and you better know how to avoid them.

You must discard most of what you hear from others, whether those in the industry or media with an agenda or well-intentioned friends and associates who seek to advise you. Most of them are part of the disconnected society whose apathy has helped facilitate the retirement risks you face. You must commit to taking control of your own small universe. You should be aware of the macroeconomic and political variables that impact your universe but your focus should remain on the concentrated area around which your life and your priorities revolve. You can't merely pull off the road and wait for conditions to improve or the dangers ahead to repair themselves. You must find a reliable navigation system to safely guide you past the obstacles that threaten your road to retirement.

An apathetic malaise threatens to envelop our society. As someone saving for retirement, if you fail to take personal responsibility, your options in retirement will be severely limited. You can allow yourself to be swallowed up by the converging traffic or you can take control, find an alternate route and shape your future as you wish it to be.

In this book, I hope to open your eyes to the need to redefine your retirement and help you find strategies to make it happen.

> *The death of democracy is not likely to be an assassination from ambush. It will be a slow extinction from apathy and indifference."*
>
> —ROBERT M HUTCHINS

CHAPTER TWO

THE HIDDEN GENERATION

The new reality for the Baby Boomer generation is that the vast majority will continue to have some form of employment after age 65. Some will work because they can't imagine not doing something productive after decades of earning a living. A larger number will work because their financial situation demands it.

A recent survey of American workers age 60 and older by the Transamerica Center for Retirement Studies found that 82% of those responding expect to either keep working past the age of 65 or don't plan to retire ever.[1]

The 2014 Retirement Confidence Survey from the Employee Benefit Research Institute shows a long-term trend in the rise of workers' expected retirement ages. Back in 1991, 31% of workers said they expected to retire between ages 60 and 64. By 2014, this figure dropped to 18%. The same survey found that 49% of older workers left the workplace earlier than planned, often for reasons beyond their control, such as health problems (61%), downsizing or plant closure (18%) and to provide care for a spouse or family member (18%).

---

1   Charisse Jones, "Traditional Retirement Possibly Becoming A Thing Of The Past," USA Today 5 May 2015.

This is consistent with several other surveys of workers and not at all surprising given the widespread concern over inadequate retirement savings. Indeed, 62% of the workers in the Transamerica survey saying they plan to delay retirement, citing the need for income or health insurance as their primary reason.

According to the Administration on Aging, as of 2013, the latest year for which data is available, there are 44.7 million Americans age 65 years or older. These aging Baby Boomers—the majority of which say they expect to continue working past the traditional retirement age—represent a staggering challenge for the country's economy and political leaders.[2]

Born in 1946, the first Boomers turned 65 in 2011; the last will reach 65 in 2029. By then, the total population of Americans over 65 will swell from 44 million to 70 million, a 75% increase. For most of the next two decades, the senior population will be growing at well over 3% per year. That's faster than total U.S. population growth, and faster than real gross domestic product (GDP) growth in recent years as well.[3]

In 1970, when the oldest of the Baby Boomers were in their early 20s, the total publicly held national debt was about $283 billion, or about 28% of the gross domestic product (GDP). By the end of 2014, the national debt had swelled to more than $18 trillion, exceeding the economic output of the entire country. Our country's younger generations will be paying this debt down for decades.

---

2   Steve Vernon, "Will Boomers Really Be Able To Work Past 65?" CBS News 6 Jan 2015.
3   governing.com

However, a Pew Research survey finds little appetite among Boomers for deficit reduction proposals that would take a bite out of their own pocketbooks. For example, 68% of Boomers (compared with 56% of all adults) oppose eliminating the tax deduction for interest paid on home mortgages; 80% (compared with 72% of all adults) oppose taxing employer-provided health insurance benefits; and 63% (compared with 58% of all adults) oppose raising the age for qualifying for full Social Security benefits.[4]

BOOMERS NOT ALL ALIKE

While lumping everyone born between 1946 and 1964 into a single category may be convenient for academics and historians, it's an inaccurate assessment. There are significant differences between those born in the mid-forties and those who arrived 10 or 15 years later. According to social marketer William Schroer, the societies they grew up in were strikingly different. As a result, their experiences, attitudes, values and behaviors were different.

The "Early Boomers," born between 1946 and 1954, were influenced by the Kennedy and Martin Luther King assassinations, civil rights movements and the Vietnam War. They enjoyed robust economic opportunities and were largely optimistic about the potential for America and their own lives.

The "Late Boomers," born between 1955 and 1964, were the first post-Watergate generation. They abandoned much of the optimistic views and trust in government the Early Boomers had. The younger members of the Late

---

4   2010, PewSocialTrends.org.

Boomers did not have the benefits of the Early Boomer group as many of the best opportunities were taken by the larger and earlier group. Both the Late Boomers and the succeeding Generation X suffered from this long shadow cast by the Early Boomers.

The following decade, 1966-1976, spawned Generation X. Often referred to as the "lost" generation, this was the first generation of "latchkey" kids, exposed to lots of day-care and divorce. With the lowest voting participation rate of any generation, Gen Xers were quoted by Newsweek as "the generation that dropped out without ever turning on the news or tuning in to the social issues around them." The group is often characterized by high levels of skepticism, "what's in it for me" attitudes and a reputation for some of the worst music to ever gain popularity.[5]

As retirement approaches for Late Boomers, they represent a *Hidden Generation*. Their priorities, interests and behaviors may be an amalgam of Early Boomers and Gen Xers, but now in their fifties and sixties, they are confronted by financial issues unlike other generations.

Like the first regiments of Army Rangers hitting Omaha Beach on D-Day, retirement for Late Boomers will be more difficult than expected. They will be the first modern generation to retire without employer pension guarantees. They will also be the first group of retirees relying on less than 2.5 taxpaying workers to support each Social Security beneficiary. Two of the three legs of the traditional retirement stool—Social Security and defined benefit pensions—may now be broken or gone.

---

5   William Schroer, "Generations X,Y,Z and Others," The Social Librarian.

How Many Workers Support One Social Security Retiree?

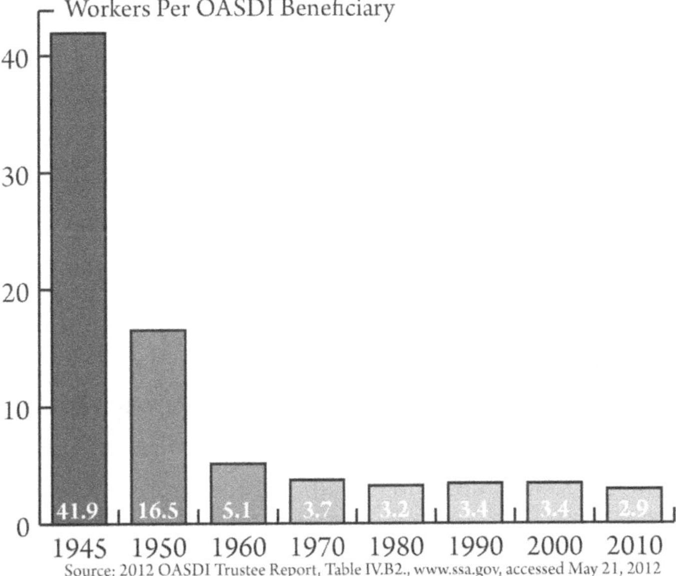

Source: 2012 OASDI Trustee Report, Table IV.B2., www.ssa.gov, accessed May 21, 2012

I was born in 1964 and so demographically, I'm categorized as a Baby Boomer. But I have little in common with those born in the forties. They are now retired and collecting Social Security. Among them are the last recipients of company-sponsored pensions. I will not receive a guaranteed pension and I am unlikely to collect the same level of Social Security benefits as the first wave of retired Boomers. I am part of the Hidden Generation, the one that doesn't get much attention because as soon as the conversation moves past Baby Boomers it skips to Gen X. Our Hidden Generation needs a separate identity because we're going to have a unique set of retirement issues.

The possibility exists that Social Security benefits as we know them may not exist 10 or 15 years from now. An increasingly large portion of our workforce is composed of immigrants who are not assimilating into the system.

Those who are paid "under the table" do not pay into Social Security and Medicare. It's suspected that much of what is earned by undocumented flows out of the country via the underground economy. It's estimated that some $26 billion was sent to Mexico as tax-free remittances by illegal aliens living in the U.S. in 2014. There is widespread acknowledgment that the problem exists but finding a solution remains problematic.

A SYSTEM FAILING

The system is unsustainable in its current iteration but not even the "experts" can agree on when it will become insolvent. Politicians continually administer band aids where major surgery is called for, and the issue is kicked further down the road to the next administration, which will no doubt do the same thing. The proverbial Social Security "lock box" was opened during WWII and seemingly never closed again. Money originally intended for our retirement was used to support other government spending and now, instead of 40 people paying in for each beneficiary, we are approaching just two.

To a large extent, it is an immigrant issue. As a nation, our birth rate has continued to drop over the past few decades. It has not exceeded replacement level since 1972 and reached an all-time low in 2013. Today, immigration is the largest factor contributing to population growth.[6] We need more new legal workers coming into the country and contributing to the system but we need to do it in an orderly and controlled fashion. We are dependent upon the

---

6   Wilson Beck, "Wakeup Call From Mexico," MuchoPress 2009

new people but we can't even agree on how to assimilate them. We are politically and socially inept at the worst possible time.

The nation is on a dangerous trajectory in terms of sustaining retirement benefits. Social security is a pay as you go program. We need legal—not illegal—immigration; we need those people coming in behind us to contribute to the system if it is to survive.

Longevity is a huge contributing factor to the problem. The typical life span in America has increased significantly over the past 30 years. Life expectancy after age 65 has grown from 15.2 additional years in 1972 to roughly 20 years today. Healthy Baby Boomers are likely to live even longer. "They could live to be 95 easily," says George Schofield, a developmental psychologist and author of *After 50 It's Up to Us*. While this longevity bonus will give Boomers more time to pursue their passions and leave their mark on the world, it's also additional years of retirement that need to be financed. "They are going to have to find a way to make their income last a lot longer than the earlier generations did," Schofield says.[7]

According to governing.gov, today's elderly "Silent Generation" retirees, currently in their 70s and 80s, are fairly well off.[8] Indeed, relative to younger households, present-day retirees are more financially comfortable than at any time in history. This is a generation that, for the most part, played by the rules and saved scrupulously. They were

---

7   "U.S. Immigration, Population Growth, and the Environment," susp. org.

8   Neil Howe, "What Makes the Boomers the Boomers?" Governing Sept 2012.

able to retire on generous defined benefit pension plans and got to cash out their home and retirement assets before the 2008 crash. Federal data released earlier this year show that, for the first time ever, households headed by people age 75 and over have a higher median net worth than any younger age bracket.

Yet this elder affluence is fading fast as successive waves of Boomers turn 65. There is a pronounced, predictable shift in retirees' overall socioeconomic situation, including a decline in household net worth and pension assets, and a relative decline in pre-retirement income. As a result, Boomers will be in increasingly greater risk of ending up in poverty or on the brink of it.

There's a persistent myth that Baby Boomers have a lot of wealth. They don't. Even before the Great Recession, Boomers weren't very well positioned for retirement. In 2007, just before the housing bubble burst, older households (between 55 and 64) had a median net worth of $266,000, according to data from the Federal Reserve. By 2010, the nest eggs of Americans approaching retirement had shrunk dramatically, falling to $179,400—a 33% drop.[9]

Another factor impeding the Hidden Generation, as well as the generations following it, is the rise in adult children living with their parents. Currently, 30.3% of 18 to 34 year-olds are living with a parent, according to data from a Census release called *Young Adults: Then and Now.* In 1980, roughly 23% of those 18 to 34 were living with a parent who was deemed the householder. In 1990, the percentage

---

9   Emily Brandon, "The Youngest Baby Boomers Turn 50," US News 16 June 2014.

living with their parents increased to 24%. In 2000, the number dipped to 23% but in 2009-2013 it reached the highest level recorded in the dataset: 30.3%![10]

RESPONSIBILITY SHIFTS

With the dramatic shift from guaranteed defined benefit pension plans to defined contribution 401(k) plans, individuals are now responsible for their own retirement benefits. Employers and government have pushed the risk back on the taxpayer. Whereas previous generations were able to maintain their lifestyle in retirement investing in bonds or CDs, that's no longer the case in today's zero percent interest rate environment. Hidden Generation retirees are being squeezed through a financial funnel into the market's risky proposition. The financial services industry and a compliant media tell people to keep their money in the market and everything will be fine. But every few years, the market plummets and it becomes obvious that everything is not so fine. The market is a risky place. The influence peddlers—financial product marketers, politicians and the media—may not have your best interests at heart.

All these elements—longevity, Social Security, pension responsibility shift—now converge as the Hidden Generation of 60 million plus Late Boomers is about to flood into retirement.

Despite overwhelming evidence to the contrary, all this data doesn't mean the problems can't or won't be corrected. Someone may have the courage to forge a solution. I am unwilling, however, to wait and see if that unlikely

---

10   CNSnews.com 17 Feb 2015.

circumstance occurs. What about you?

If someone ultimately takes responsibility and finds a solution, terrific: we'll get more than we expected. If not, let's not allow ourselves to become impoverished victims in retirement, relying on a reverse mortgage or the generosity of our children to see us through.

In the chapters that follow, I'm going to discuss why investors, including members of the Hidden Generation, have found it so difficult to accumulate sufficient personal retirement savings. I'll suggest strategies to help meet the challenges of financing your retirement without abandoning your lifestyle or forgoing the realistic pleasures you envision for the future.

> *I am very concerned about the millions of Baby Boomers who are counting on the stock market to deliver them a safe, sound, long retirement. I am afraid the Baby Boomers who are counting on the stock market are in trouble."*

> — ROBERT KIYOSAKI

CHAPTER THREE

BIASES GET IN OUR WAY

We've never had more resources and done less with them.

The unending torrent of information available through the internet and mass media should be a boon to investors, but it hasn't worked out that way. People have more information but seem somehow less educated when it comes to investment decision-making. One reason why could be that all this data simply overwhelms investors and so they end up confused and uncertain. Another possible explanation is that despite the avalanche of knowledge propelled at us, we remain victims of our own behavioral biases that get in the way of clear thinking and cause us to abandon reason and logic.

Some behavioral biases are cognitive, tendencies to think in ways that deviate from rational thinking or good judgment. Other biases are more emotional, causing us to act upon our feelings instead of factual data.

There is substantial research to support the influence of behavioral biases on our decisions, including our financial conclusions. Tversky and Kahneman did some pioneering work in behavioral finance in the 1970s.[11] In

---

11   Amos Tversky and Daniel Kahneman, "Judgment under Uncertainty: Hueristics and Biases," Science 27 Sept 1974 pp1124-1131.

addressing why people cling to certain beliefs, the authors conclude that "...people rely on a limited number of heuristic (empirical) principles which reduce the complex task of assessing probabilities and predicting values to simpler judgmental operations...which sometimes lead to severe and systemic errors."

Researchers have identified dozens of behavioral biases. Let's examine some of the more common ones as they relate to how people make investment decisions.

ANCHORING

Anchoring is the tendency to use an existing belief as a reference point for making future judgments. It occurs when investors allow a single or specific piece of information to control their decision-making process, often basing their decisions on the first source of information to which they are exposed, such as the initial purchase price of a stock.

People with an anchoring bias have a tough time changing their perception, despite new information to the contrary. Anchoring is one reason why an early life experience will control how we feel about something well into our adult years. If we are taught a certain group of people are slow witted or untrustworthy, that bias is likely to embed itself permanently in our mind. If I failed to buy Apple stock when it sold for $20 a share, I can't bring myself to buy it at 95, even if all indications are that the stock it is likely to go much higher.

In his book, *Predictably Irrational*, Duke Psychology Professor Dan Ariely discusses how evaluating decisions based primarily on the comparison of similar alternatives while ignoring dissimilar alternatives consistently impairs human judgment. He argues that, "We not only tend to compare things with one another but also tend to focus on comparing things that are easily comparable—and avoid comparing things that cannot be compared easily."[12]

Psychologist Dr. Linda Sapadin describes the anchoring effect as a "cognitive bias that influences you to rely too heavily on the first piece of information you receive. And it's not just a factor between the generations. Stores use it all the time to convince you to buy."

Suppose you are shopping for a new BMW. The list price is $75,000 but after two hours of haggling, you agree to a "reduced" price of $69,500. You believe you negotiated a great deal because your "anchor basis" was the original $75,000 price.

DISPOSITION EFFECT

The Disposition Effect is a bias where investors credit their successes to their own innate abilities and ascribe their losses to uncontrollable circumstances or external factors. Here investors are more likely to sell a stock that has gone up in value than one that has gone down in value.[13]

The behavior can be costly. Disposition investors who need cash and are forced to sell stock are more likely to sell one that has appreciated, even though liquidating a losing stock would provide a capital gains tax benefit. A 1985 Shefrin and Statman study of aggregate mutual fund

---

12   Dan Ariely, Predictably Irrational: The Hidden Forces that Shape Our Decisions, New York, NY: HarperCollins 2008.

13   Hersh Shefrin and Meir Statman, "The Disposition to Sell Winners Too Early and Ride Losers Too Long," The Journal of Finance 1985.

purchases and redemptions supports the disposition effect, revealing that more redemptions occur during good stock market months than poor ones.

Politicians often provide us with a textbook example of the disposition effect. When referring to their sponsorship of popular legislation, they speak in the first person. ("I was the first Congressman to bring this critical issue to light.") When asked about a failed policy or a reversal of position, you might hear something like, "The conditions at the time caused many of *us* to believe the legislation would effect a different outcome."

We've never been more educated and yet more confused.

CONFIRMATION

The tendency of investors to search for evidence that confirms an opinion they have already formed and to ignore anything that contradicts that opinion is called a Confirmation Bias.

An example is the ongoing war of words among scientists regarding global warming. Those who believe in it are unswerving in their advocacy, evidence to the contrary notwithstanding. And vice versa.

This tendency to place greater credence on data that supports one's beliefs than to contrary data can be particularly damaging for investors whose beliefs may be little more than biases.

If you believe that during a full moon there is an increase in admissions to the emergency room where you work, you will take notice of admissions during a full moon but be inattentive to the moon when admissions occur during other nights of the month. A tendency to do this over time unjustifiably strengthens your belief in the relationship between the full moon, accidents and other lunar effects.[14]

> *Your assumptions are your windows on the world. Scrub them off every once in a while, or the light won't come in."*
>
> — ISAAC ASIMOV

EXTRAPOLATION

Many investors tend to extrapolate recent events into the indefinite future. They make predictions based on unfounded conclusions about what has previously occurred. This bias causes investors to abandon their long-term strategy and hinder their ability to make sensible decisions.

The effect of extrapolation was in full force after the market collapse of 2008. The S&P 500 nosedived during the year, its worse performance since 1931 amid the Great Depression. Equity investors ran one another over in the stampede to safety. Tens of billions of dollars were pulled from equity funds in the last quarter of 2008 alone, most of that money going into bank accounts and money market funds yielding 1% or 2% annually.

Extrapolation can, of course, be used to argue both for impending doom or future prosperity—sometimes based on the same data.[15]

---

14   Robert Todd Carroll, "Confirmation Bias," The Skeptic's Dictionary 1994.

15   Tom Murphy, "Ruthless Extraolation" physics.ucsd.edu 26 June 2012.

OUTCOME

Outcome bias is the tendency to make a decision based on the desired outcome rather than on the probability of that outcome. Investors judge their decision making based on the results of the process rather than the quality of the process itself.

Conducting experiments on the subject in 1975, researcher Ellen Langer found that people were less willing to sell their lottery tickets when they had chosen the ticket number themselves than when the numbers had been chosen for them.

**"If the economy is moving so slow,
why does our money go so fast?"**

Drunk drivers are an example of the outcome bias in its most frightening and potentially destructive form. They no doubt know it's a bad idea to try to drive while impaired, especially the first time that they do so. But if they manage to get to their destination without an accident, they are more likely to drive drunk in the future. The outcome of their action had no negative consequences so they begin to believe there is nothing wrong with repeating the action. Critical evaluation of the decision making process is more likely to deter the drunk driver in the future than focusing on the outcome.[16]

AVAILABILITY

We live in the information age. When investors place more weight on information that's readily available or easily recalled, it's referred to as an availability bias. A frequent source of this bias is the media, which can influence investor behavior by devoting extensive coverage to attention-grabbing news. Investors tend to be more strongly influenced by what is most recent or dramatic.

An example would be passing a gruesome roadside accident and responding by driving more cautiously for a while until the effect wears off and you return to your normal driving habits.

We recently heard from an anxious client who is approaching retirement. The night before, he and his wife had watched a financial news show where a guest analyst said retirees should withdraw 4-5% annually. Of course, it doesn't always work that way. There are many considerations to assess before making that kind of determination, but the client was made so nervous but what he heard on TV that he wanted immediately know how much he could spend.

---

16   Nick Kellingly, "Outcome Bias — Not All Outcomes are Created Equal," Interactive Design Foundation.

"There are situations in which people assess the probability of an event by the ease with which instances or occurrences can be brought to mind. For example, one may assess the risk of heart attack among middle-aged people by recalling such occurrences among one's acquaintances."[17]

FAMILIARITY

According to researchers Fox and Tversky (1995), "When people are offered two alternatives, they prefer the one that they are familiar with." This bias holds true for stock selection when investors are better informed about familiar securities versus ones that they are not. Comfort with the familiar and ambiguity about the unfamiliar leads individuals to prefer investing in securities they believe they know more about.

Researchers Grinblatt and Keloharju argue that familiarity may also have its roots in considerations such as the distance of the stock's headquarters from the investor or similarity of the investor and company's culture.

In a 2002 study, Ning Zhu, assistant professor of management at the University of California, Davis argues that local bias—the tendency to invest in nearby investment alternatives—and home country bias may be a function of the same underlying driving factor, familiarity bias. The results confirm that both *institutional and individual* investors exhibiting a higher degree of the bias tend to hold stocks of companies with nearby headquarters.[18]

---

17   Amos Tversky and Daniel Kahneman, "Availability: A heuristic for judging frequency and probability," Cognitive Psychology 1973.
18   Bülent Tekce, "What Factors Affect Behavioral Biases?" unicreditanduniversities.eu.

Another example of familiarity bias is the penchant by investors to buy shares in the companies they work for or companies whose products they purchase or admire. Of course, the danger is becoming overweighted in the company stock and risking being under-diversified.

OPTIMISM

We normally regard optimism as a positive trait but excessive optimism can cause investors to overestimate the frequency of favorable outcomes and underestimate the frequency of unfavorable outcomes.

**"I retire on Friday and I haven't saved a dime.
Here's your chance to become a legend!"**

For example, individuals underrate the chance of getting divorced, being in a car accident or suffering a major illness, while they expect to live longer than others, overestimate their success in the work force and believe that their children are especially talented.[19]

Excessive optimism is similar to overconfidence although one can be pessimistic yet confident about it. Psychologists have shown that the bias causes individuals to overestimate their knowledge, underestimate risks and exaggerate their ability to control events. It occurs frequently in investment decision-making because security selection is a difficult task, the type of activity at which people exhibit the greatest overconfidence.

WE ALL DO IT

We know what to do but we don't do what we know.

We all harbor behavioral biases, a fact universally agreed upon by academics, psychologists, researchers and virtually everyone in the financial services industry. Yet despite widespread awareness, most investors say they do not believe they personally exhibit these traits. This inability to acknowledge our individual behavioral biases dooms many investors to a lifetime of ill-advised financial decisions and the resulting lack of adequate retirement funds.

When behavioral finance expert Daniel Kahneman was asked what could be done to overcome behavioral biases, he remarked, "Very little; I have 40 years of experience with this, and I still commit these errors."

Given we are all susceptible to counterintuitive and potentially destructive biases, logic tells us that the first step in overcoming them is acknowledgment. Once we accept our foibles, we can go about the business of

---

19   Dr. Mirela Malin, "Psychological biases and decisions making in finance — Pitfalls to avoid" MBA White Paper for Griffith University

overcoming them, or at least not letting them take control of our financial future. We know what to do; we have only to do it.

> *Overoptimism and overconfidence tend to stem from the illusion of control and the illusion of knowledge."*
>
> — JAMES MONTIER

CHAPTER FOUR

401(K): THE PROMISE UNFULFILLED

"A corporation's responsibility is to the shareholders, not its retirees and employees. Companies are doing everything they can to get rid of pension plans and they will succeed."

—BEN STEIN

One of the most misconstrued financial products ever created is the 401(k). Unlike the defined benefit plans it replaced—pensions that guarantee retirement income— the 401(k) is not a pension and guarantees nothing.

Over the past three decades, there has been a seismic shift from traditional employer-sponsored pension plans to defined contribution plans, most of which are 401(k) plans wherein employees are responsible for investment decisions. Developed back in the 1980s, the 401(k) was originally created for the benefit of executives in companies that already provided pension plans for lower level employees.

When their defined benefit plans were frozen or eliminated, employees were told that the new 401(k) plans would allow them to take control of their retirement future. Companies painted a pretty picture but it wasn't as if employees had a choice. The 401(k) became their only choice. Despite lacking meaningful investment training or guidance, workers now had to decide for themselves how much they needed to save for a comfortable retirement and what investment vehicles would best do the job.

Hyped as offering employees newfound control over their financial future by employers, politicians, the mutual fund industry and an unrelenting blitz by the advertising industry, employees were dragged into a new arena, as prepared for the battle as were the ancient Christians awaiting the lions.

Investments and
Financial Planning

"I have a diversified retirement portfolio: 25% down the drain, 40% out the window, 35% gone with the wind."

In a 2013 *Frontline* interview, Teresa Ghilarducci, director of the Schwartz Center for Economic Policy Analysis at the New School for Social Research, noted that, "Most people don't know that the 401(k) product is toxic. The behavior towards the 401(k) product is also toxic because no one has been responsible for providing a safe product. Congress has not put itself out as a responsible actor. Employers were told, 'It's up to your employees to choose.' The banking industry and the mutual fund industry said 'Trust us.' So the reason workers don't know that their 401(k) products and the choices that they make won't yield enough return and that they're paying high prices is because the products are dangerous, and nobody regulates them."

A 401(k) is not an automatic product; it has to be steered and watched. And that's part of the problem. Even if you contribute regularly, choose appropriate investments and do everything else well, you are still subject to occasional market severe declines that can eviscerate 20 or 30% of your savings. If you have the misfortune of experiencing one of these market drops in the first couple of years of your retirement, you're in big trouble. The culprit is longevity. We are living so much longer today and that means we need a lot more retirement savings to sustain our extended lifetimes. The longer you live, the more market drops you will be exposed to. Longevity can be a portfolio assassin.

For 2016, the maximum employee contribution is $18,000 for those under age 50 and $22,000 for workers over age 50.

Some companies cap 401(k) contributions at levels below IRS contribution limits for reasons such as cost, accounting or an outdated plan document.

CRYPTIC BY DESIGN

The 401(k) is one of the most mysterious financial products ever devised, and it's that way intentionally. Plans typically offer an array of investment choices, dominated by mutual funds and index funds. Plan participants rarely have a good understanding of the price, quality or fees associated with the funds they choose, nor are they aware of the dangers inherent in their choices.

As Ms. Ghilarducci notes, "One of the worst aspects of the 401(k) industry is the conflict of interest. The 401(k) industry took fees from customers, paid lobbyists to go to Congress to say, 'you don't need fee transparency. People won't really understand it. Let the market thrive, and then through competition, the fees will just be appropriately priced.' And so that was the story year after year when the Congress tried to expose the fees."

When Congress passed The Pension Protection Act of 2006, requiring companies that had underfunded their pension plans to pay higher premiums to the Pension Benefit Guaranty Corporation, it drove the final nail into the coffin of defined benefit plans. The Act continued the regulation of the traditional pension system while providing a virtual free pass to the 401(k) industry. If the self-directed 401(k) is such a beneficial (excuse the pun) retirement product, why is it that public sector employee unions stridently refuse to convert their workers' defined benefit bonanzas into 401(k) plans? Because given the choice, employees always prefer a guaranteed benefit to a hopeful aspiration.

That hopeful expectation was shattered in the financial crisis of 2008 when virtually every 401(k) participant was made acutely aware of how risky managing one's own retirement plan can be. But plunging retirement fund values were overshadowed by the more immediate crisis of rising unemployment and home loss. While the politicians swung into action to protect homeowners and mortgage lenders, they summarily ignored workers whose plummeting 401(k) values saw their retirements jeopardized.

I believe another element at work during and immediately after the 2008 financial crisis was the mutual fund industry's lobbying clout, which may have forestalled any attempts to regulate the 401(k) industry and the mutual funds that made up the lion's share of most participant's plans. Ultimately, Congress passed legislation requiring the industry to make their fees more transparent.

FEE FEST

In my opinion, the 401(k) remains as one of the most egregious scams in modern finance. The reason is fees: stacks of needless charges piled willy-nilly, one on top of the other. Expensive mutual funds are finally ceding ground to index funds and ETFs, leaving 401(k) "management" fees as the last great rip-off in retirement saving.[20]

401(k) fees vary, often depending on the size of the plan. The median expense ratio of a plan with a small number of employees is typically much higher than that for the plan of a large company. The ratio incorporates the administrative, investment management and marketing fees charged to plan participants. In 2010, the median expense ratio for plans with less than 100 participants was 1.29% whereas for plans with more than 10,000 participants, it was 0.43%.[21]

There are several categories of fees associated with

---

20   Mitch Tuchman, "Is Your 401(k) a Total Scam?" Forbes 19 Dec 2012.
21   Robert Hiltonsmith, "The Retirement Savings Drain," Demos.org 29 May 2012.

401(k) plans.[22]

Plan administration fees include record keeping, accounting, legal and trustee services. Some plans cover these services with investment fees deducted from investment returns. In others, they are paid by the employer or charged against the plan's assets. Generally, the more services provided, the higher the fees.

Fees for managing plan investments constitute the largest component of fees and expenses and are usually assessed as a percentage of assets invested. Plan participants pay for these in the form of an indirect charge against their accounts because they are deducted directly from investment returns. Since they are not specifically identified on statements of investments, these fees may not be apparent.

In addition to overall administrative expenses, there may be individual service fees associated with optional plan features. These fees are charged separately to the accounts of individuals who opt for these features, such as taking out a loan or executing participant investment directions.

In addition to fees for plan administration, there are fees that may be charged in connection with investment alternatives in a 401(k) plan. These fees include sales charges in the form of loads or commissions, trading fees associated with buying and selling securities. Mutual funds pay a fee each time they buy or sell one of the securities that comprise the underlying assets of the fund. These costs—which vary from year to year depending on

____

22   401(k)revenuesharing.com

the frequency with which fund managers buy and sell the funds' assets—are passed on to participants via the funds' share prices.

There are also investment advisory or account maintenance fees, ongoing charges for managing the assets of the investment fund. They are generally stated as a percentage of the amount of assets invested in the fund and can vary widely, depending on the investment manager and the nature of the investment product.

Finally, there are miscellaneous fees, a category covering services such as record keeping, furnishing statements and investment advice. These may be a flat fee or stated as a percentage of the amount of assets invested in the fund.

According to Radford University President and retirement plan analyst Robert Hiltonsmith, "The high fees that 401(k) plans charge are one of the worst aspects of these plans. Every investment option in a 401(k) charges hidden and high fees for investment management and other services."

Many 401(k) plans offer target date funds as an option. Target date funds are hybrid mutual funds that automatically reset their asset mix according to a selected time frame deemed appropriate for a particular investor. The principal value of these funds are not guaranteed at any time, including the target date.

For example, if you plan to retire in 20 years, you might buy a target-date fund that matches your time frame of 20 years. As you approach your retirement date, the fund moves its allocation to more conservative mutual fund investments and away from riskier mutual fund investments. The reallocation over a predetermined period to reflect investors' changing tolerance for risk is known as the target-date fund's glide path. The glide path sets the fund's allocation among various asset classes over time, adjusting the mix from more aggressive investments early in the life of the fund to more conservative investments as the fund matures and investors approach their targeted goal.[23]

While the average fee for any mutual fund is 0.80%, the number for target date funds is a hefty 1.08% annually. Some funds are much, much worse. Legg Mason's Target Retirement Series charges 1.47% expense ratio for the privilege of taking your money. How do they get away with it? Well, the industry promotes them as "set-it-and-forget-it" funds, thereby attracting the sort of investors most likely not to ask many questions.[24]

---

23   Lee McGowan, "The Pros and Cons of Target Date Funds," thebalance.com 31 May 2016.
24   Helaine Olen, "401(k)s are a Sham," AlterNet News & Politics 6 Aug 2013

Despite the lofty fees, a 2011 AARP Fee Study revealed that 71% of the plan participants questioned were not even aware that they pay fees to their 401(k) plan provider to maintain their account.

An employee who contributes $5,000 per year to a 401(k) plan with an annual return of 7% and no fees would earn about $469,000 over a 35-year period. However, with an annual fee of 1.5% of the account balance, the same employee would earn only $345,000 in a 35-year period.[25]

PENSIONED EMPLOYEES DO BETTER

While defined benefit pensions are almost extinct in the private sector, it's instructive to compare their historic investment returns with that of 401(k) plans. A 2011 study by Towers Watson, the global human resources consultant, found that pension plans beat 401(k) offerings by nearly 3 percentage points. Pensions made investment returns of 2.74% while defined contribution plans lost money, delivering -0.22%.

Overall since 1995, Towers Watson found defined benefit plans outperformed by 76 basis points annually (0.76%) and did so in nearly all of those years except years in which stocks boomed, such as 2009.

Part of the reason is the mutual funds in the plans studied which had weighted average expenses of 65 basis points in 2011, a drag which reduced overall returns by 31 basis points. Nearly half of the 401(k) type plans were composed of mutual funds, compared to just 14% in the

---

25   AARP Public Policy Institute. Determining Whether 401(k) Fees are Reasonable: Are Disclosure Requirements Adequate? Sept 2008.

pension plans. The consultant concluded that pension plans did a better job with less risk.[26]

The responsibility for assuring an adequate retirement income has been permanently transferred from companies to individuals. You're expected to be your own money manager because advisors like me don't have much opportunity to help you with your 401(k) until you roll it over when you change employers or retire. By then, you may be so far behind in achieving your goals that it may be too late to do much good.

I have to manage my clients' 401(k)'s from arms length. The government and your employer have said that responsibility for your retirement is on you but they have chained you to a limited menu of investment products. Your 401(k) investment options are restricted even though you are personally accountable for dealing with your longevity.

Your 401(k) has become the replacement for your pension. You regularly add money to it and manage it with minimal professional help. Occasionally, a rep from one of the companies that offer mutual funds in your plan comes by and gives you and your fellow plan participants the asset allocation pitch. You don't know exactly what fees you are paying or whether the mutual fund choices are the best you can get. This is your roadmap for a fulfilling retirement?

Bill after proposed bill has stalled in Congress because the mutual fund industry has a huge and powerful lobby. Politicians laud the need for a better architecture for 401(k) plans, including broader product selection and allowing your personal financial advisor to help you manage your

---

26   Mitch Tuchman, "Pension Plans Beat 401(k) Savers Silly – Here's Why," Forbes 4 June 2013.

biggest investment: your 401(k). But all the political pontifications come to naught.

Suppose the Agriculture Department announces a pilot program for farmers, asking each if they would rather pay a tax on the seeds they plant in the spring, or a tax on the fall harvest. Basically, that's the proposition of a 401(k) or IRA. You receive a small tax deduction up front, and you're expected to grow your field of seeds into an abundant harvest in time for your retirement, 25 or 30 years from now. At that time, the government gets a piece of that you have accumulated over the decades. Your 401(k) is the equivalent of a farmer paying a tax on his fall harvest. A scrutiny of this idea reveals its lunacy. The deductions you receive over the years while you put your money into a 401(k) may be far outweighed by the taxes due when you withdraw the money after retirement. You are told not to worry about that, however, because you will be in a lower tax bracket when you retire. How do they figure that? You may not have any more earnings after retiring, but you also won't have any deductions. Most people come to realize that in order to maintain their lifestyle, they need almost as much income after retirement as they did during their working years. Your tax bracket in retirement may actually be higher than it is now.

With a Roth IRA, there's no deduction when you put money in but also no tax on the harvest.

One thing Congress needs to move on soon is allowing a wider array of investment options, including alternative investments. Nothing should be omitted without serious consideration and analysis. One example is the use of annuities. You can find plenty of advisors who say annuities are a bad idea but like many things, annuities are neither innately good nor bad; their appropriateness within a 401(k) plan would depend on the application and individual circumstances.

Writing in the Harvard Business Review, Nobel Economist Robert Merton argues for changing the barrier to annuities in 401(k) plans: "One of the best ways to be assured of steady future income is to invest in an inflation-adjusted annuity but current 401(k) regulations do not allow deferred annuities as an investment option."

If you asked a contractor to build your home without using a hammer or screwdriver because you read some-where that they are dangerous tools, completing the con-struction would be haphazard, at best. They same thing holds true of selecting investments for your retirement plan. Never reject a product based on propaganda from someone in the mutual fund industry. In my opinion, they haven't done such a great job for 401(k) plan participants anyway.

THE 401(K) FICTION

The avalanche of retiring Baby Boomers—especially the Hidden Generation comprising those born between 1955 and 1964—likely face the unprecedented prospect of lower living standards than the generations that preceded them. Throw in the likelihood that at some point, Social Security benefits will be cut and you have an indisputable retirement crisis. The cause of this crisis can attributed to the failure of the promise of the 401(k).

Writing in AlterNet News & Politics, author Helaine

Olen notes, "The industry gets away with this because it has what amounts to a captive audience. While there is some evidence that the recent Department of Labor requirement to reveal 401(k) plan fees to participants has brought expenses down, knowledge does not leave consumers in the driver's seat. If you discover your company plan is sub-par—the fund choices are poor or the expenses are too high—all you can do is complain to your human resources department and hope they decide to change plans. Employees simply have to take what is given to them."

"I think the biggest frustration people have with the 401(k) is that employers are no longer taking on the responsibility to pay you for 25 or 30 years after you stop working for them (which is essentially what it means to guarantee someone a retirement income). That's just the way it is. And in reality, the era of corporate sponsored retirements was actually quite short. It spanned about 30 years, from 1950 to about 1980. For the most part, companies completely underestimated what it would cost to assume this liability for you. Once they figured it out, they gave it back to you."[27]

One of the three legs of the traditional retirement stool—the guaranteed benefit pension—has been pulled out from underneath you and replaced with a do-it-yourself product dubbed the 401(k). The sales pitch that company stock and a limited array of mutual funds will get you safely to your retirement goals may be a false promise. If you rely on a 401(k) and dubious future Social Security

---

27   Charlie Farrell, "What's Wrong with the 401(k)?" CBS Moneywatch 4 Oct 2010.

payments to fund your post-working years, you may wake up at age 65 to find your working years are far from over.

Responsibility for funding a satisfying lifestyle in retirement has been dropped in your lap. Don't drop the ball. You know what to do; now do what you know.

> *The do-it-yourself version of pensions is a flop, as many Americans have painfully learned."*
>
> —WILLIAM GREIDER

CHAPTER FIVE

SELF SECURITY

"The public has lost faith in the ability of Social Security and Medicare to provide for old age. They've lost faith in the banking system and in conventional medical insurance."

—RON CHERNOW

Back in the early 1930s, the Great Depression was in full force. Millions of Americans had no jobs. Many of those lucky enough to have employment didn't earn enough to feed their families. It was in this environment that newly elected president Franklin Roosevelt saw fit to create landmark legislation known as *The Social Security Act of 1935.*

The original description of the term "social security" meant a program intended to provide help for the poor, the physically disabled, the mentally ill and the elderly. Obviously, that definition got lost in translation over the following 80 years.

A 1936 government pamphlet on Social Security explained, "After the first 3 years—that is to say beginning in 1940—you will pay and your employer will pay 1.5 cents for each dollar you earn up to $3,000 a year.

Beginning in 1943, you will pay 2 cents, and so will your employer, for every dollar you earn for the next 3 years. Finally, beginning in 1949, twelve years from now, you and your employer will each pay 3 cents on each dollar you earn, up to $3,000 a year."

Here's the kicker: "That is the most you will ever pay."

Had Congress lived up to its promise, our current maximum Social Security tax would be less than $100 a year instead of over $6,000. The Social Security Act of 1935 would have never been enacted had Americans back then known that we'd be subject to a $6,000 tax.

In a 1937 U.S. Supreme Court case, *Helvering v. Davis,* the Court held that Social Security was not an insurance program saying, "The proceeds of both employee and employer taxes are to be paid into the treasury like any other internal revenue generally, and are not earmarked in anyway."[28]

And so it became apparent early on that the money individual Americans and their employers donated to the Social Security account was destined to be used not specifically to fund the retirements of the people from whom the money was extracted, but rather for any purpose Congress decided was necessary.

Pension payouts were to begin in 1942. After thirty or thirty-five years the federal government was to reimburse the payouts. But when President Roosevelt learned that the federal government would owe the fund more than a billion dollars by 1970, he ordered his Secretary of the Treasury to insist that under no circumstances would the

---

28   Econfaculty.gmu.edu

federal government assume any financial responsibility. The plan had to be made self-sustaining.

The result was an epic change in the structure of the Act. Contributions would now be doubled their original amount to a total of 6% within twelve years. This effectively transferred the entire burden of old-age dependency after 1942 to the backs of the young workers and their employers. Since businesses would pass the bulk of the increased levy on to consumers, it meant that the young employees—in their dual role of workers and consumers—would bear the major cost of the accumulated problem of old-age dependency.

Writing in *The Nation* in 1935, Abraham Epstein noted, "The old-age contributory insurance plan is fraught with many dangers. Enormous reserves, estimated at more than $10,000,000,000 by 1948 and at more than $40,000,000,000 by 1980 are contemplated. These will create a stupendous problem of investment. Experience everywhere indicates that politicians will hardly be able to keep their hands off such easy money."[29]

At the time Social Security was enacted, the average life expectancy in America was 61.9 years, fully three years short of when individuals could apply for benefits. It was never intended to be the primary source of retirement income but rather a safety net against poverty. Over the years, the public's perception of Social Security has changed dramatically. Today, *Social Security is the principal source of family income for nearly half of older Americans,* according to AARP. Twenty-four percent of those aged 65

---

29   Abraham Epstein, "Social Security Under the New Deal," The Nation 1935.

and over live in families that depend on Social Security benefits for 90% or more of their income. Another 26% receive between 50 and 90% of their family income from Social Security.

The fact that so many Americans now rely on government welfare for so much of their retirement income is chilling. It also illustrates the seismic shift that has taken place, transferring financial responsibility from employer-funded pensions to individuals and their 401(k)s.

"A two dollar stock sounds like a perfect investment for me. After all, how far down can it go?"

The generation spanning the Great Depression through the first wave of Baby Boomers is riding out the last wave of the pension era. There are still employer pensions out there but companies aren't starting any new ones. The beneficiaries of these remaining pensions are the last to rely on the three legs of the retirement stool: pensions, Social Security and personal savings. They will tell you that the checks from Social Security and their pension—not their personal savings—are the two most important legs of their stool because they know they can count on receiving them every month. Given the diminishing ratio of workers to retirees, that Social Security check may not be a certainty for much longer, and it certainly is not assured for the back end of the Boomer generation and those who follow.

I used to conduct private seminars for various professions, such as nursing. Invariably, the topic professionals were most interested in discussing was Social Security. I invited an expert on the subject—a former executive in the Social Security system—to make a presentation and answer questions. I could not believe some of the things he said. For example, a man who married three times could have two ex-wives as well as his current wife all collecting benefits based on his lifetime earnings. This may sound like fraud but it's perfectly legal. And that's just one example.

Here's another from Boston University Professor Larry Kotlikoff, appearing on an episode of *PBS Newshour* in March, 2014. The bizarre example he cites would be hilarious if not for the fact that it is entirely possible, not to mention legal.

I thought I'd provide this outrageous tale of William Cooper Caldwell Gigolo to illustrate another peculiarity of our Social Security system.

William Gigolo worked not a day in his life, but instead lived off the relatively high earnings of three lovely wives—Sarah, Sally and Suzie. William is now 62 and has been single for two years. He's a handsome devil (looks like Paul, actually). He refers to the three "S" gals as "My exes."

William's very happy to have lived off of each of his exes, helping himself to half their assets when they divorced. In each case, William waited until their 10th anniversary, chose a romantic restaurant, and over dessert, announced he was filing, not for Social Security, but for divorce.

Why wait 10 years? Because William knew that he had to be married 10 years, and not a day less, to qualify for divorcée spousal benefits and, when an ex died, divorcée survivor benefits, on his spouse du jour (well du decade).

Since your ex has to be at least 62 for you to collect spousal benefits, William was careful to marry at least one ex older than himself. This wife is Sarah, who is 64 and was the lowest earner. The next highest earner was Sally, who is 60. Suzie is the baby at only 56, but she earned more than the other exes.

To maximize his lifetime Social Security benefits, William files for a divorced spousal benefit at 62 and starts to collect half of Sarah's full retirement benefit, but reduced by 30% because he takes it early. Then, after two years, when Sally is 62, William files for a divorcée spousal benefit based on Sally's earnings record.

And why not? Since he's now eligible to collect on two exes, he can file for benefits on both. He won't get two divorcée spousal benefits—just the larger of the two. But Sally's full retirement benefit is larger than Sarah's, so he flips to hers. And here's the lovely thing from William's perspective: he'll be able to collect half of Sally's full retirement benefit, but reduced by only 13.3%, not 30%! Why? Because the *reduction of benefits based on one spouse's earnings record doesn't carry over to collecting on another's.*

William's cash-out plan is working. But there's a part three. In six years, when Suzie reaches 62 and William is 68, he flips onto Suzie's earnings record and starts collecting a completely unreduced divorcée spousal benefit since he doesn't start collecting this particular benefit (which exceeds the other two) before he reaches his full retirement age.

Is William done with his optimization? No. Let's fast forward to William's 70th birthday, which is also the day that Sally, who waited until full retirement age to start collecting her benefit, dies. Sally's full retirement benefit, while lower than Suzie's, exceeds half of Suzie's. So now William files for and begins collecting an unreduced spousal benefit on Sally's record equal to 100% of Sally's full retirement benefit.

Fast forward again. William is now 76 and Suzie dies (of a broken heart) having also waited until full retirement age to collect her retirement benefit. What does William do? He files for an unreduced survivor benefit based on Suzie's earnings record.

Fast forward one last time. William is now 88. He's met a very lovely 94-year-old named Sandra, who earned more than any of his exes and is on her last legs. William realizes that he can marry Sandra and, after nine months, qualify for survivor benefits on Sandra's earnings record. Presto, he whisks Sandra off to Las Vegas for a quickie marriage and, nine months to the day of their nuptials, Sandra falls, breaks her hip, and heads north by north.

William leaves the funeral early in order to get to the local Social Security office before it closes and file for a full (unreduced) survivor benefit on Sandra's account.

This appears to be William's last Social Security play, but he's still a handsome devil and is on Match.com checking out his options.

Post script: This is no way to run a railroad, let alone our nation's Social Security system.

In their 2015 report on the Social Security system's finances, the trustees said, "Social Security's Disability Insurance (DI) Trust Fund now faces an urgent threat of reserve depletion, requiring prompt corrective action by lawmakers if sudden reductions or interruptions in benefit payments are to be avoided. Beyond DI, Social Security as a whole as well as Medicare cannot sustain projected long-run program costs under currently scheduled financing."

The report goes on to say that the combined trust funds that help pay old age and disability benefits are likely to run out by 2034, the year when today's 48-year-olds reach full retirement age.

With over 60 million beneficiaries, Social Security is America's biggest, most popular government program, and its actuaries have the crucial job of telling us how far it is from hitting fiscal icebergs. The trillion-dollar program's importance is such that its' forecasts are closely watched by policy experts. Among them is Gary King, a prominent Harvard University political scientist who, with colleagues, published a sharply critical 2015 study calling the actuaries' forecasts "systematically biased and overconfident."

Published in both the *Journal of Economic Perspectives* and the *Journal of Political Analysis*, the report revives long-standing complaints that government analysts employ research methods that are antique and opaque compared with the statistics and open-source data analytics powering today's successful scientific and business enterprises. In the global-positioning-system era, these critics say, Social Security is steering itself by sextant and dead reckoning. Notes King, "This is the single largest government program with the most intense politics, but not a single person in or out of government, in or out of academia, or in or out of the commercial world has ever managed to fully replicate the Social Security Administration's forecasts."[30]

We've never had more resources and done less with them.

---

30   Bill Alpert, "Social Security's Predictions: Off by $1 Trillion," Barron's 9 May 2015.

Social Security is a pay as you go system. Taxes from today's workers are used to fund the benefits of today's retirees. Politically, Social Security is a third rail. Neither political party wants to approach the problem for fear of voter backlash, but the problem must be resolved and soon. It's not as if the issue has emerged overnight. The government knew about the approaching shortfall as far back as the 1970s, but instead of stabilizing the system with necessary, if painful, changes, they kicked the proverbial can down the road. Seeing the demographics of increasing longevity, an expanding retiree population and a shrinking contributing workforce, their solution was to shift fiscal responsibility from employers (pensions) to individuals in the form of the 401(k). The move only delayed—and likely exacerbated—the eventual outcome. It's taken almost 50 years to reach the crisis point but it has, at last, come to indisputable fruition.

> *Should any political party attempt to abolish social security, unemployment insurance, and eliminate labor laws and farm programs, you would not hear of that party again in our political history."*

—DWIGHT EISENHOWER

Today, the political class has no more appetite for taking on the issue than their counterparts did four or five decades ago. While 78 million Baby Boomers flood into retirement, our government is dysfunctional at the worst possible time. It's not that they are out to get us; it's simply that they have no credible solutions.

Jagadeesh Gokhale, senior fellow at Cato Institute, writes that Social Security officials have long been misdiagnosing the program's financial condition. Whether this reflects poor judgment, incompetence or deliberate misdirection seems impossible to determine.

The program's total unfunded obligations—$20.5 trillion according to the report—grow at an interest rate that is larger, on average, than the productivity-plus-population-growth formula that determines growth of the payroll tax base. Calculations based on micro-data sources of demographics and economic behavior suggest that the program's long-term financial shortfall is about 50% larger than the trustees are letting on."[31]

Psychotherapist Dr. Michael Hurd offers an interesting perspective on Social Security:

The whole premise of Social Security and Medicare is that people will not take care of themselves, plan for their retirement or purchase health insurance in a free market. Therefore, it follows, that government must take care of this for them.

If that's true, then how or why are people expected to purchase their own houses? Or their own groceries? Or their own automobiles? If people are too helpless to plan for and purchase insurance, then aren't people too helpless to do other equally important things?

This is where the inherent dishonesty of the whole Social Security and Medicare scheme is exposed. If people are able and willing to provide for these services, they can and

---

31 Jagadeesh Gokhale, "Trustees' Projections Mask Social Security Shortfall," Politico.com 30 Apr 2012.

will do so. If they cannot, then no government system of health care and retirement insurance, on such a massive scale, would ever be possible. The scam in the whole thing isn't a Ponzi scheme so much as an unwillingness to admit that Medicare and Social Security are, in fact, welfare schemes.

There's no easy and overnight solution. The only likely solution is to admit these programs were a terrible moral and economic mistake, and to phase them out over a period of several decades. This will not happen because politicians will not tell the truth, and Americans will not face it. The truth will hit home, however, once benefits start getting trimmed or eliminated for those the politicians consider less deserving. The debate won't be about facing facts, but about which group should be allowed to keep getting these benefits and which groups should have to give them up. That's when it will really get interesting.

To this day, many people believe the myth that the government puts the money paid into Social security into an account so it is there to pay them back with interest when they retire.

The fact is that taxes paid by people who are working today provide the benefits for people already retired. The Social Security taxes you pay during your working years pay for the benefits received by your retired parents. The Social Security taxes your children pay will support your Social Security benefits in retirement.

Here are a few more Social Security issues to consider:

- Social Security alone is unlikely to provide a comfortable retirement. The average Social Security retirement benefit in 2015 is $1,328 a month. Can you live on $15,936 per year? The maximum benefit for someone at full retirement age (currently 66) is $2,663; for those who wait until age 70 to retire, the maximum is $3,501 a month. That sounds better, but if you qualify for the maximum benefit, you were earning over $100,000 during much of your career, and you're probably not going to be happy living on $42,000 a year.

- The pundits have declared that inflation is dead, and now they worry about deflation—an actual decline in the cost of living. It's true that last year the average Consumer Price Index inflated by only 1.6%. But remember the 1970s and 1980s, when inflation more typically came in at 5%? In one year, 1980, it went up over 13%. Even in the early 2000s, inflation chugged along at closer to 3%. So $100 from the year 2000 is today worth only about $72. If you retire at age 66 and expect to live another 20 years, $100 will then be worth only about $64, or maybe less.

- The stock market has been doing great since 2009, and produced a lot of wealth for retirees who have invested in stocks and mutual funds. But as the first two months of 2016 illustrated, the markets can reverse themselves rather quickly. Also recall 2008 and 2001, when the stock market took terrible tumbles. The stock market is a good place to invest for the long term, but it can sting your finances pretty painfully in the short run.

Several recent polls have found that Baby Boomers express an interest in working after they retire, usually as a consultant or in a part-time job. This may pan out for some, especially those who are able to keep options open with their old company. But while many employed people say they want to work in retirement, a significantly smaller number of current retirees are actually working. Why the discrepancy? Jobs are not that easy to get for people over 65. And as we hit our 70s, we may find that we don't have the interest or stamina to continue in the labor force.[32]

We've never been more educated and yet more confused.

A Wall Steet Journal article on July 16, 2011 notes that while negotiating the debt ceiling talks in 2011, President Obama famously played to grandma's Social Security fears, saying in an interview that, "I cannot guarantee that those (Social Security) checks go out on August 3 if we haven't resolved this issue because there may simply not be the money in the coffers to do it."

WHATEVER HAPPENED TO THE TRUST FUND?

That's the fund that, according to our politicians, is holding all those Social Security taxes that workers pay. Why can't Congress or Mr. Obama dip into that $2.6 trillion cash hoard to pay benefits until the debt-limit business gets sorted out? After all, as White House budget director

---

32   "Don't fall for these retirement fallacies," U.S. News, 10 Mar 2015.

Jack Lew put it in a February USA Today op-ed, "Social Security benefits are entirely self-financing."

Not quite. As everyone in Washington knows, the trust fund contains not cash but IOUs. Payroll taxes don't go to some vault in Fort Knox, and they certainly aren't invested. When Social Security runs a surplus, Congress spends the money immediately on something else and then the government claims it owes a debt to itself. Where the money will come from to pay these IOUs is anybody's guess—though Mr. Obama is hoping it will be higher taxes. As Bill Clinton's budget director put it in 1999, "Trust fund balances only exist in a bookkeeping sense."

A Cato Institute commentary compared Social Security to Otto von Bismarck's welfare state in Germany, calling it a "Ponzi scheme, with new contributions used to pay off earlier investors." Author Marc Rudov states that, "Social Security is irreversibly insolvent." In 1950, the worker-to-beneficiary ratio was 16.5 to 1. In 2010, that ratio is almost 2 to 1. Notwithstanding the political nonsense, Social Security's failure is rooted not in actuarial anomalies, but in the violation of immutable psychology: people succeed only when they are responsible for their own decisions and actions. When government manages your life, it will fail—and therefore, you will fail."[33]

In 2012, Goldman Sachs CEO Lloyd Blankfein (a Democrat) was interviewed on "Sixty Minutes" by CBS reporter Scott Pelley:

Blankfein: You're going to have to undoubtedly do something to lower people's expectations—the entitlements

---

33   Marc H Rudov, "Social Security: Successful Failure," Dec 9 2010.

and what people think that they're going to get, because it's not going to—they're not going to get it.

Pelley: Social Security, Medicare, Medicaid?

Blankfein: You can look at history of these things, and Social Security wasn't devised to be a system that supported you for a 30-year retirement. So there will be things that, you know, the retirement age has to be changed, maybe some of the benefits have to be affected, maybe some of the inflation adjustments have to be revised. But in general, entitlements have to be slowed down and contained.

Andrew Eschtruth, associate director for external relations at the Center for Retirement Research at Boston College and co-author of the Center's booklet "The Social Security Fix-It Book" says, "The interesting thing is that it's pretty straightforward to fix. Not easy, but compared to solving the longer-term problems facing Medicare, it's clear. Either Social Security must pay somewhat less in benefits or Americans will have to pay more in taxes...or some combination of the two."

For the Hidden Generation—the tail end of Baby Boomers—now approaching retirement, Social Security income is no longer a leg of the stool that can be relied upon. Responsibility has been thrust upon the individual and as such, you had best plan pessimistically when it comes to Social Security. In fact, I might suggest you forget social security and plan instead on self security as a replacement. For self security, you will need multiple avenues of guaranteed income. To do that, you must investigate alternative investments.

We will do that in a following chapter.

"*Since Social Security faces a large gap between what it promises younger workers and what it can afford to pay them, private savings will likely need to play a larger role in retirement planning for younger workers.*"

—RON LEWIS

CHAPTER SIX

ACCELERATED BUBBLES: THE NEW PARADIGM

"Prices are going up. Unemployment continues to go up. And we have not had the necessary correction for the financial bubble created by our Federal Reserve system."

—RON PAUL

In decades past, economic cycles were permitted to play out, independent of government intervention. As the country experienced alternating booms and busts, the business cycle responded with vacillating expansions and contractions. Things occurred more or less naturally and it was not unusual for a market cycle to last 15 or 20 years.

Enter Alan Greenspan as the Chairman of the Federal Reserve in 1987. Suddenly, Fed policy shifts from advocacy to aggressor. Greenspan believes the Fed should play a more active role in attempting to smooth out the cyclical fluctuations. He institutes a soft monetary policy, supported by artificially low interest rates. Over time, the markets and the business community come to rely on this continuing policy of near-zero short-term interest rates. It's a dangerous assumption.

In October 1987, shortly after Greenspan assumed

office, the *New York Times* reported, "...the morning after the stock market crashed, the Fed offered this one-sentence statement: 'The Federal Reserve, consistent with its responsibilities as the nation's central bank, affirmed today its readiness to serve as a source of liquidity to support the economic and financial system.'"

It did the trick. The market stabilized, and the United States economy kept growing for four more years. Eleven years later, when a crisis in emerging markets seemed to threaten the booming American economy, the Fed cut interest rates three times, successfully containing the damage. When the dot-com bubble was collapsing in 2001, it did the same, less successfully.

In each case, Fed officials argued that they were not focused on trying to prop up the market for its own sake, but were trying to keep the economy on an even keel despite market turmoil."[34]

Voila! No more recessions!

---

34   Neil Irwin, Economic View, "Fed's 3 Mandates: Price Stability, Jobs and ... Wall Street?" New York Times 26 Feb 2016.

We've never had more resources and done less with them.

In the pursuit of fighting bubbles, the Fed has inadvertently created what appears to be a perpetual credit bubble, comprised of a series of bubbles following one another in rapid succession.

Sad to say, a lot of people like it. Investors hope for an economy with sustained growth, so the Fed is committed to providing it by creating an uninterrupted credit bubble. Fed Chairman successors Ben Bernanke and Janet Yellen have continued the low interest rate policy, which now appears to be a permanent Fed dogma, regardless of the long-term consequences.

But the consequences couldn't be more ominous for Hidden Generation Boomers now approaching retirement. Despite the Fed's intervention—or perhaps because of it—the economy continues to crawl along at a sluggish pace with artificially depressed interest rates support it.

Again, is this accelerated bubble environment something new or history repeating itself? I doubt anyone really knows the answer to that question. During my quarter century in financial services, I've seen several bubbles occur, spurred by economic, terrorist or financial events, some with near catastrophic impact. In 1994, we experienced the Latin American monetary devaluation. My brother, who was selling Latin American bonds on an institutional desk at the time, found himself unemployed virtually overnight. A similar threat occurred just two years later when Vietnam and other emerging market countries were forced to devalue their currencies. Next came the tech bubble of 1999, followed by the tragedy of 9/11 and the financial meltdown of 2008. Are we facing another imminent threat to our country's wellbeing?

We've never been more educated and yet more confused.

How can anyone confidently invest for retirement in this environment? We don't even know if this is an anomaly or the new normal. There's no question we are in unchartered waters. In the past, we experienced long periods of time—in some instances, a decade or two—of unremitting growth. Is what we are now experiencing the new paradigm or just the tip of the iceberg that hasn't yet crushed us? The one thing we do know is that the Fed has assumed a much more assertive role in manipulating the market.

Because of the fact that the Fed has maintained such a low interest rate for so long, it's really crippling for seniors to generate income in retirement.

You have this confluence of all of these things and we're taking away tools. We're taking away ways to have a safe retirement as we're going to live longer. We keep reducing the ability to finish the job or protect ourselves. At the same time, we're allowing nano-second trading. We have so much manipulation in the markets. People have been known to spread rumors just so they can short the market. The bad guys know how to use technology to their advantage.

Given that employers have essentially removed themselves from the task of guaranteeing retirement income, and the government continues to unsuccessfully wrestle with sustaining a failing Social Security system, responsibility for retirement income has been draped upon the shoulders of individual Americans. With fixed income vehicles paying less than the rate of inflation, stocks are the only option for small investors to try to keep pace.

Meanwhile, a malfunctioning and disconnected government stands by idly while the Fed dictates policy. It's as though a game is being played but no one is playing on a team. It's become an individual sport with everyone doing their own thing to take advantage of the rules, or lack or them. As always, the individual investor gets left behind.

IT'S A DIFFERENT GAME TODAY

Past generations were not forced to rely on the stock market for their income replacement in retirement. Our parents and grandparents counted on the three-legged stool of pensions, Social Security and personal savings. In decades past, retirees and those approaching retirement had access to treasuries or bank products that paid 5,6,7 percent or more so they were not reliant on equities to outpace inflation and provide adequate income. They had other, safer outlets for effective risk management. As the wealthy late Gene Autry used to say, "I'm not as interested in the return on my money as I am in the return *of* my money.

But the investment options available to generations past have largely been taken away from today's investors approaching retirement. One leg of the stool—guaranteed pensions—has been sawed off by corporate and government interests. A second leg—Social Security—is wobbling and threatens to break. The Fed has created an interest rate environment where fixed income products return rates are so low even a 2% annual rate of inflation renders them a losing proposition. And now individuals are told they can "take charge of their own financial future" by investing in a risky arena: the equity markets, where they little if any chance of achieving the portfolio growth necessary to generate sufficient retirement income. Unlike other areas of modern life where greater flexibility and more options are available—such as food choices, healthcare and information access—today's investors seeking safe income replacement options face harshly limited choices. They have been thrown into a deep, water-filled pit. Their options are to tread water until interest rates rise, drown, or wait for the inflation alligators to eat them.

"Forty years a client and I'm still
a small investor!"

Unlike past generations, bonds offer today's retirees no relief. Bond prices and interest rates are an inversion, like a seesaw on a playground. When interest rates go up, bond prices go down. If interest rates are at a low point—as they have been for a decade as a result of Fed policy—bond prices remain high. The further out on the yield curve, the greater the sensitivity to interest rate movements, even small ones. Should the Fed reverse policy and raise interest rates, investors would be hit with a double whammy: low yields and the inability to liquidate their bonds without suffering a loss of principal.

When the equity market experiences heavy volatility, investors instinctively rush into treasuries. Seniors nervously jump into treasuries despite their low yield and susceptibility to huge downside price risk. When the Fed nudged interest rates up a mere 25 basis points in December 2015, the equity markets suffered an immediate 10% correction. The Fed has boxed itself in. If it raises interest rates, it triggers a market plunge, not to mention it must also apply a cost of living adjustment on Social Security benefits, something the country cannot afford.

What the Fed has created is an environment of uncertainty and distrust. The government has told investors, "You are responsible for building your own retirement home and it will need a substantial foundation to withstand uncertain economic weather...and oh by the way, the government will be collecting rent on your property so make sure you do a good job of construction so we can rely on that income. Sorry but we can't give you the tools needed for proper home construction because we had to sell them off for cash, but here are a few primitive tools to get you started. Good luck building your retirement home. Oh yes, almost forgot: hurricane season is fast approaching so be careful you don't get caught outside working when it hits.

That's an analogy of what's been going on in recent times. We need a safe retirement, but we have to achieve it without the proper tools. There are no pensions or adequate fixed income tools available and the Social Security tool is broken and may not be repairable. You have only a highly dangerous tool—the equities markets—for most of the work but be careful because it's unpredictable and has caused injuries to many others.

As an investor approaching retirement, you can't stick your head in the sand and hope to get lucky. You have to prepare for the possibility of any contingency because the odds of escaping the current environment unscathed and realize the American dream are not in your favor. The seemingly perpetual bubble we find ourselves in may or may not be the new normal. The traditional income replacement vehicles have been whittled down to one unsavory choice. Whatever the new paradigm, it's unlikely to be a positive development for the Hidden Generation approaching retirement and those that follow.

> *The Federal Reserve - all of them - could be sitting on a barrel of dynamite, and then pouring gasoline on top of it, and then light a cigar with matches, throw the match into the gasoline, and then not notice that there is any danger."*
>
> —MARC FABER

CHAPTER SEVEN

IMPEDIMENTS

Earlier, you read about the biases that inhibit us from making sound investment decisions—destructive behaviors that can be overcome once we acknowledge their existence and learn to ignore their toxic influence.

Biases are internal obstacles, but there are also external forces that inhibit us from making sound investment decisions, among them the media, government and the financial services industry. Just as you must overcome your personal biases and behaviors, you must also conquer the caustic external influences.

MEDIA

> *What the mass media offers is not popular art, but entertainment which is intended to be consumed like food, forgotten, and replaced by a new dish."*
>
> —W. H. AUDEN

The influence of the mass media on the investing public can hardly be overemphasized. As mentioned previously, the incessant noise it generates plays a pivotal role in distorting the realities of retirement investing.

The rationale for 24/7 financial news media is to keep viewers and listeners tuned in by appealing to their most basic emotions: fear and greed. The teasers that precede commercial breaks compel viewers to "stay tuned because you won't believe..." Commercials sponsored by major brokerage firms and insurance companies portray a euphoric retirement, thanks to their expert investment guidance, just before the mandatory disclaimer, "past performance is not an indicator of future results" appears in microscopic script at the bottom of the screen.

> *Let advertisers spend the same amount of money improving their product that they do on advertising and they wouldn't have to advertise it."*
>
> —WILL ROGERS

Investment firm analysts and mutual fund managers appearing as guests are prodded to offer stock tips. I wonder whether these represent meticulous research or are merely stocks the guests wish to move off their trading desks.

The talking heads are prodded to make predictions as to whether the market will sink or soar, whether a stock is overpriced or undervalued, whether interest rates will rise or fall, and a host of other financial and economic queries.

Viewers are advised to take a long-term approach to retirement investing, then fed a nonstop diet of "breaking news" and nanosecond reporting on every twitch in the markets.

We've never had more resources and done less with them.

This is the mass media, keeping viewers tuned in so they will see the advertisements of the sponsors who enable these shows. I see it as an incestuous relationship presented under the guise of sound financial advice. It continues because it evidently works, just like the commercial for the "recently uncovered cache of gold coins" that has been running for over a decade.

Investments and Financial Services

"No, you haven't made buckets of money yet. Your initial investment was used to purchase buckets."

In a published paper titled, "Do Ads Influence Editors? Advertising And Bias In The Financial Media," the authors conducted a five-year analysis of the recommendations of the publications that received the most mutual fund advertising dollars. They discovered "a positive correlation between a mutual fund family's advertising expenditures and the probability that its funds are recommended in the publication. Named in the study were highly respected media, including *Money Magazine, Kiplinger's Personal*

Finance and *SmartMoney.*

The authors summarized by saying, "While we consider several alternative explanations, the robustness of the correlation leads us to conclude that the most plausible explanation is that personal finance publications bias their recommendations—either consciously or subconsciously—to favor advertisers.[35]

All of this propaganda causes more stress for those in or approaching retirement. They become confused and paralyzed by information overload. They don't know what to do so they do nothing and hope for the best. Or they overreact and do something foolish.

---

35   Jonathan Reuter and Eric Zitzewitz, "Do Ads Influence Editors? Advertising And Bias In The Financial Media," Quarterly Journal of Economics Aug 2005.

GOVERNMENT

Our government appears to have become completely non-functional. Perhaps the fact that over the past few years, Congress has averaged less than 130 days of work per year, or roughly 2.5 days per week in session. Not bad for a salary of $174,000 per annum. Reform is sorely needed but whether it ever occurs is doubtful.

The country has been ensnared in a low-growth economy, averaging around 2% annually for the past decade. Given its heightened role in recent years, investors have come to expect the Fed to play a major role in GDP growth. But whether intentional or not, the Fed has merely served as a cover for a Congress and Administration unwilling to do their job, that being to engage our arduous tax code and its deleterious effect on business and the economy.

At 39.1%, the United States has the highest corporate income tax rate among the 34 industrialized nations of the Organization for Economic Cooperation and Development (OECD).[36]

When pharmaceutical companies Allergan and Pfizer sought to merge in what is now known as an inversion deal—where a U.S. company moves its tax base to a lower tax environment—the Treasury Department of the Obama Administration issued an overnight regulation removing the tax benefits Pfizer hoped to gain from the deal with Ireland-based Allergan. This despite the fact that the two companies constructed the deal around the

---

36   OECD Tax Database, Table II.1 – Corporate income tax rates: basic/non-targeted (last updated May 2014), http://www.oecd.org/tax/tax-policy/tax-database.htm.

laws Congress had previously set for companies looking to move to a foreign domicile. Instead of seeking solutions to the problem of American companies moving overseas to avoid our onerous tax burden, I believe the Administration crushed the merger by imposing harsh new regulations.

I agree with Steve Forbes and others who contend that a high corporate tax rate stifles growth, which translates into fewer jobs, less expansion, less R&D, less new products and lowered shareholder value. For investors, it means lower returns on the stocks of those companies.

> *The investor is bombarded with staggering amounts of information, staggering amounts of stimuli that are designed to get the investor to buy and sell and trade, to do exactly the wrong thing, to create excessive profits for these intermediaries that aren't acting in the investor's best interests."*

—DAVID SWENSON

It appears that the previous Administration pretty much left Wall Street to govern itself, which led to systemic abuse that helped fuel the market crash of 2008. Under the present Administration, the pendulum seems to have swung wildly in the opposite regulatory direction.

I doubt people will suddenly begin to govern themselves judiciously. Greed is a fearsome instinct and some simply can't resist getting out of control and taking advantage of the system. Unfortunately, we now seem to have an environment where legitimate business transactions are quashed by an overly zealous government that has created its own problems. Perhaps what we need is a government that can focus on the problems and find workable solutions.

We know what to do but we don't do what we know.

In 2016, the Department of Labor (DOL) imposed a fiduciary rule changing the way retirement investment assistance is provided to Americans. I consider this regulation to be oppressive for the financial services industry.

According to the U.S. Chamber of Commerce, "Although the final rule accommodated a few concerns expressed by commenters, many of the critical fixes to the Fiduciary Rule called for by the U.S. Chamber of Commerce remain unaddressed or were made worse in the final rule. These include important issues, such as whether the final rule discriminates against small businesses, limits the availability of investment education, and substantially increases litigation risk to the detriment of savers and the retirement system."[37]

The rule affects the advisor/client relationship for every 401(k), IRA and every rollover or distribution to or from either. The rule ostensibly would allow advisors to continue to sell and service small business plans without absorbing or passing on higher costs. But like most government regulations, the law of unintended consequences surfaces and the opposite effect occurs. "The final regulation will still require most small business plan advisors to change their business models, incur major new transition and compliance costs, and in many cases, subject themselves to serious litigation risks. This cost will be paid by small businesses and their employees in the form of higher

---

37 www.uschamber.com/sites/default/files/documents/files/u.s._
chamber_-_assessment_of_the_dol_fiduciary_rule.pdf

costs, reduced choices, and less access to advice."[38]

I believe the government has discouraged professional financial advisors from helping lower and middle class investors because there's no longer any profitability in serving that group of people. I doubt many brokers will touch those accounts now; the risks are too high with no compensatory benefit. Those the government allegedly seeks to protect will suffer the worst. Unfortunately, that is what we have come to expect from government: inadvertently hurting the people they propose to help.

> *The government solution to a problem is usually as bad as the problem."*
>
> —MILTON FRIEDMAN

The new regulation retains the DOL's class action litigation enforcement mechanism, which, given the subjective conditions, will only encourage frivolous litigation. The upshot of this new regulation will be to deprive smaller 401(k) plans of competent financial counsel as the restraints and risks of litigation will discourage most advisors from taking on smaller clients. It will also mean many smaller broker/dealers will be out of business, eliminating jobs, reducing competition and making it more difficult for smaller businesses to get competent financial advice for their 401(k) plan participants.

The government may not be the source of all our financial woes but its lack of focus and partitioned special interests make it near impossible to get anything constructive accomplished. Our problems continue to fester and grow

---

38   Ibid

worse, and that's not a promising outlook for those near or in retirement.

> *Pressed to identify useful financial innovations created during the past quarter-century, Paul A. Volcker, former Federal Reserve Chairman and recent chairman of President Obama's Economic Recovery Board, could single out only one: 'The ATM.'"*
>
> —JOHN BOGLE, THE CLASH OF THE CULTURES:
>
> INVESTMENT VS. SPECULATION

FINANCIAL INDUSTRY

In his book, *Unconventional Success*, investment legend David Swensen offers incontrovertible evidence that the for-profit mutual-fund industry consistently fails the average investor. From excessive management fees to the frequent churning of portfolios, the relentless pursuit of profits by mutual-fund management companies harms individual clients. Perhaps most destructive of all are the hidden schemes that limit investor choice and reduce returns, including "pay-to-play" product-placement fees, stale-price trading scams, soft-dollar kickbacks, and 12b-1 distribution charges.[39]

When mutual funds started to come under attack in the early 2000's, the financial services industry realized they had to do something to reinforce their position that everything was just fine and that the product remained a

---

39   David Swenson, Unconventional Success (New York: Simon & Schuster, 2005).

good choice for investors, in particular for retirement savings. So they began creating hybrid products, like the fund of funds, a mutual fund comprised of other mutual funds, and target date mutual funds.

"If you factor in the money you didn't lose on the investments you didn't make, you're doing quite well!"

The fund of funds, in my opinion, is a highly inefficient investment product. It's typically made up of the other mutual funds the issuer already holds or of various hedge funds. Investors pay two levels of fees: management fees and performance fees. The fees may be tolerable if the fund's performance warrants them, and indeed, some hedge fund sectors will typically outperform the markets in a given year. The key is knowing which hedge funds will do that, not unlike knowing which equity mutual funds will outperform the market during a given year. To me, that's speculation and not worth the risk. When the funds fail to outperform, the result may be higher costs and more cluster.

Investing in a collective investment scheme may increase diversity compared with a small investor holding a smaller range of securities directly. Investing in a fund of funds may achieve greater diversification. According to modern portfolio theory, the benefit of diversification can be the reduction of volatility while maintaining average returns. However, this is countered by the increased fees paid at both the fund of fund level and at the level of the underlying investment fund.[40]

Target date funds automatically rebalance the mix of equities and fixed income, transferring more weight towards fixed income as the date for beginning withdrawals grows nearer. These funds have gained considerable popularity because on the surface, they seem to make sense for those approaching retirement. But just like the fund of funds, there are serious issues. The concept takes a blanket approach, assuming everyone approaching retirement is in a comparable financial situation, which is obviously not the case. Those who have a pension, or expect to continue working in retirement, or who have other income-generating investments might do better to retain a higher percentage of stocks. Those more likely to begin immediate withdrawals upon retirement may require a heavier weighting in bonds. The problem here is that with interest rates at historic lows, fixed income returns may not even keep pace with inflation. Having a disproportionate ratio of fixed income in one's retirement portfolio could be

---

40 Wikipedia.

a serious mistake. Reacting to low fixed income returns by shifting more assets into equities is the typical response, but that may mean taking on more volatility and greater risk, something retirees may not be comfortable doing.

Another dubious strategy is the trust. Retirees might be advised to put all their assets into a trust to avoid probate. But revocable trusts can be challenged by unhappy heirs and in some states, it's actually easier to challenge a trust than a will. Many people mistakenly believe a trust protects their assets from creditors, an assumption that is not always valid.

I recently met a retiree who, after attending a trust seminar, allowed an attorney to transfer the funds from his million-dollar IRA into a trust. What the attorney failed to tell him—assuming the attorney even knew the fact—was that the transfer created a taxable event. And this was an experienced attorney, not someone who just passed the bar exam.

We've never been more educated and yet more confused.

It may not be in the financial industry's interest to embrace—much less initiate—any significant changes in the way it does things. The transformational shift from guaranteed pensions to individual responsibility via 401(k) plans serves the financial industry, and specifically mutual funds, very well.

Millions of working people add money to the mutual funds in their 401(k) plans every week. What the industry calls money management I would call money marketing because the focus may be on the amount of money flowing into the funds, not what the fund managers choose to do with it.

The mutual fund business continues to be about money through the door. Investors may unwittingly be paying for professional babysitting. An astonishing 86% of active fund managers failed to beat their benchmarks in 2014, according to Dow Jones. Further, roughly 89% of those fund managers underperformed their benchmarks over the past five years and 82% did the same over the last decade.[41]

As for passive investing using ETFs and similar vehicles, it's a bit like putting your portfolio on autopilot. In good weather, it's wonderful; in inclement weather, you would rather have someone behind the wheel.

It's difficult to beat the index because of the fees and costs associated with mutual funds. This industry is obligated to disclose most—but not all —their fees. There are fees and transaction costs investors may not be unaware of. In my opinion, the concept of buying and holding mutual funds simply does not work.

> " The mutual fund industry has been built, in a sense, on witchcraft."
>
> —JOHN BOGLE

---

41   "86% of investment managers stunk in 2014," CNN Money 12 Mar 2015.

CHAPTER EIGHT

RETIREMENT RESPONSIBILITY IS YOURS

"You cannot escape the responsibility of tomorrow by evading it today."

—ABRAHAM LINCOLN

I hate to make others uncomfortable when discussing their retirement, but all too often I have to remind someone that long ago, I cautioned them about waiting too long to start saving for retirement.

If you start early and have a sensible plan, retirement planning can be a breeze. That's not blue sky; I've helped hundreds of people do it. The problems arise when people procrastinate. There are few things more frustrating than to have someone you like ask you what they can do now that retirement is just a few years away and they haven't saved enough...or anything...to provide income for their later years.

Now what?

The conversations with people when they still have time to start saving can be difficult because as an advisor, I'm telling them something they don't want to hear, even when they know it's the truth. They don't want to change;

they want an easier path to a comfortable retirement. They fantasize they can wait until they are older, have less financial obligations, are making more money...etc. Then maybe I can find a way to help them generate double-digit returns for a few years and everything will be fine when they want to retire.

It doesn't work that way. Most people know it but they still deceive themselves. And it's sad because I know what the problem is and how to solve it. But the solution is not what they want to hear. It's especially difficult for people to face reality when much of the underpinning for a safe retirement has been chopped out from underneath them. The company pension they hoped for when younger never happened or disappeared. The Social Security contributions they have been making for 30 years may only provide a fraction of the retirement income they anticipated. Their 401(k) and IRA accounts took a drubbing in 2008-09. They saw half their money evaporate and in panic, pulled out of the market. They watched as the market rallied and regained everything it lost while they parked their money in fixed income products earning even less than the meager inflation rate.

Frustrated and confused, they now see retirement approaching like a late afternoon express train and wonder what they can do.

While this scenario tends to be the exception rather than the rule for the clients I work with, there will always be those who refuse to take responsibility for their financial futures and suffer the consequences. I hope you are not one of them but if you are it's time to acquire a sense of urgency and accept that you will have to make some changes. It doesn't matter whether your current situation is of your own making or you are the victim of a corporate downsizing, a stagnant economy, or simply because you waited too long to take action, you must accept that the government has largely abandoned you to your own devices when it come to providing retirement income. You will have to make changes, perhaps drastic and painful changes, but they are necessary. You must make sure, however, that they are the right changes.

It's natural to recall better days and rationalize what a great time that was. Things have changed, as they always do, and from a retirement perspective, not for the better. A lot of people can't accept that.

I'm not promoting gloom and doom, but you have to accept that retirement risk has been transferred to us as individuals. That's a cold hard fact and it isn't likely to change anytime soon. Big business and the government has invested too much money and political capital to do an about face. Guaranteed benefit pensions are a thing of past glory days, as is a fully funded Social Security system. The equity markets have become increasingly volatile and bonds and CDs pay little more than burying your money in the backyard.

How do you offset all these impediments? Jump into the market and hold your breath? Some in the financial industry tout the "safety" of a buy and hold strategy using mutual funds. I call it "buy and hope."

This is a critical issue that I spend a lot of time talking about with my clients. We are in a dramatically different environment than previous generations. We have to adjust to what has changed by changing how we think and invest.

With two legs of the retirement stool sawed off, you have to prop up your retirement stool with an approach that employs not one or two, but multiple buckets—multiple retirement income stream sources.

You have to shift your thinking. Retirement planning now means portfolio growth must take a back seat to income. Today, I would much rather be receiving dividends than trying to find something to put my money into that might grow. I want to be rewarded now, not some time in the future. The stock market is a frighteningly risky place; bonds are in a bubble, yielding next to zero and run the risk of collapsing values if interest rates rise. All of this is converging on you as you try to plan for retirement. Way too many people are ignoring the obvious, hoping somehow things will work their way out, or the government will find some magical solution. Given the lack of leadership and the seeming inability of the two political parties to agree on anything, it's doubtful you can count on that. Our leaders no longer fix anything in this country until it absolutely breaks down. They are crisis managers when necessary but they are not forward thinkers.

> *When government accepts responsibility for people, then people no longer take responsibility for themselves."*
>
> —GEORGE PATAKI

I'm someone who is thinking forward. It's one reason why I wrote this book. If you understand that you are responsible for your own safe retirement, you better be a forward thinker too. If you are in your late 40s or 50s, things are only going to be incrementally more difficult when you get to retirement age. You need to start thinking forward.

David Swenson, Chief Investment Officer of the Yale University endowment fund, is another forward thinker. Swenson understands the reality of market volatility, unlike most individual investors who fear it. I regularly talk to people who abandoned the market in 2008 and have been afraid to reenter it since. They are emotionally devastated. They have also missed out on the market recovery that would have allowed them to recapture much or all of what they lost a decade ago.

We've never been more educated and yet more confused.

EARLY LOSSES ARE LETHAL

When people retire, they expect—or hope—the markets will perform according to the models they have seen, typically using historic market returns. If a couple retired in 2013 and used the S&P 500 as a benchmark to project how their portfolio might perform in the coming years, they would see that the average annual return of the previous 20 years was 10.08%. They might logically project that into the future are feel pretty good about withdrawing 4-6% annually to provide retirement income.

What they might not notice is the discrepancy in performance from year to year, from a high of +37.58% in 1995 to a low of -37% in 2008. The overall annualized return may look promising but years with big losses can throw that average annual return number right out the window.

Consider the following chart that depicts the frequency

of the market taking major hits.

Year	S&P 500	Average Annual Returns	5-year Annualized Returns	10-year Annualized Returns	15-year Annualized Returns	20-year Annualized Returns	25-year Annualized Returns
1992	7.62%	10.34%	15.88%	16.17%	15.47%	11.33%	10.56%
1993	10.08%	10.33%	14.55%	14.93%	15.72%	12.76%	10.52%
1994	1.32%	10.20%	8.70%	14.38%	14.52%	14.58%	10.98%
1995	37.58%	10.55%	16.59%	14.88%	14.81%	14.60%	12.22%
1996	22.96%	10.71%	15.22%	15.29%	16.80%	14.56%	12.55%
1997	33.36%	11.00%	20.27%	18.05%	17.52%	16.65%	13.07%
1998	28.58%	11.22%	24.06%	19.21%	17.90%	17.75%	14.94%
1999	21.04%	11.35%	28.56%	18.21%	18.92%	17.88%	17.25%
2000	-9.11%	11.05%	18.33%	17.46%	16.02%	15.68%	15.33%
2001	-11.89%	10.71%	10.70%	12.93%	13.74%	15.24%	13.77%
2002	-22.10%	10.21%	-0.59%	9.34%	11.48%	12.71%	12.98%
2003	28.68%	10.43%	-0.57%	11.06%	12.21%	12.98%	13.84%
2004	10.88%	10.43%	-2.30%	12.07%	10.93%	13.22%	13.54%
2005	4.91%	10.36%	0.54%	9.07%	11.52%	11.94%	12.48%
2006	15.79%	10.43%	6.19%	8.42%	10.64%	11.80%	13.37%
2007	5.49%	10.36%	12.83%	5.91%	10.49%	11.81%	12.73%
2008	-37.00%	9.62%	-2.19%	-1.39%	6.46%	8.42%	9.77%
2009	26.46%	9.81%	0.41%	-0.95%	8.04%	8.21%	10.54%
2010	15.06%	9.87%	2.29%	1.41%	6.76%	9.14%	9.94%
2011	2.11%	9.77%	-0.25%	2.92%	5.45%	7.81%	9.28%
2012	16.00%	9.84%	1.66%	7.10%	4.47%	8.21%	9.71%
2013	32.39%	10.08%	17.94%	7.40%	4.68%	9.22%	10.26%

Assuming our couple is healthy and retires at age 65, they can reasonably expect to live for another 20-30 years. That means the odds are they will experience any number of market drops of 10% or more. Given the market drops 30% an average of once a decade, they face the probability of seeing the equity portion of their portfolio suffering at least two monumental hits during their retirement. What they may not realize is what it takes to recover from a 30% plunge. If they own $500,000 worth of equities, a 30% drop would mean a $150,000 loss. It would take not 30% but a 43% gain to recoup their loss!

Retirement income assumptions are often based on the 4% withdrawal rule established by financial advisor Bill Bengen in 1994. It proposed retirees who withdrew 4% of their initial retirement balance and adjusted that amount for inflation each year could reasonably rely on receiving that income for 30 years. It was offered as a more or less fail-safe method of ensuring a retiree would not run out of money. The theory was based on a retirement portfolio evenly split between stocks and bonds.

Market Falls By This Much	Historical Frequency
10%	Every 11 Months
15%	Every 24 Months
20%	Every Four Years
30%	Every Decade
40%	Every Few Decades
50%	2-3 Times Per Century

The strategy relies on historic asset return assumptions, which promise a 30-year failure rate of just 6%. But this optimistic failure rate rises sharply if real rates of return decline. Bengen's calculations didn't take into account an extended period of historically low interest rates, as we have experienced in recent times, nor did they account for a nasty little glitch known as the *sequence of returns*.

If your portfolio suffers significant losses during the early years of retirement, all the rosy 30-year projections of the 4% withdrawal rule go out the window. A study published in 2014 showed that continued low interest rates such as the country has experienced over the previous five years would cause the projected failure rate to soar to 57%! The study also stated that, "Because of sequence of returns risk, portfolio withdrawals can cause the events in early retirement to have a disproportionate effect on the sustainability of an income strategy." The summary concluded that the success of the 4% rule may be a historical anomaly and that "clients may wish to consider their retirement income strategies more broadly than relying solely on systematic withdrawals from a volatile portfolio."[42]

As PayPal founder Peter Thiel puts it in his 2014 book *Zero to One*, "Statistics doesn't work when the sample size is one."

An easy way to understand sequence of returns is to compare identical portfolios generating the identical average rates of return over an extended period. This we did in figure 8.1, which shows two portfolios with an identical beginning balance of $500,000. The first tracks the actual S&P 500 return for 15 years with an average rate of return of 4.25%. The second reverses the returns for the same period. As you can see, after 15 years, the two portfolios have identical balances.

| | Actual S&P 500 | | S&P 500 Reversed | | Avg Rate of Return | |
| | BEGINNING BALANCE | HISTORICAL RETURN % | BEGINNING BALANCE | RETURN % | BEGINNING BALANCE | RETURN % |
YEAR						
01	$500,000	(9.1)	$500,000	13.7	$500,000	04.25
02	$454,500	(11.9)	$568,500	32.4	$521,250	04.25
03	$400,415	(22.1)	$752,694	16.0	$543,403	04.25
04	$311,923	28.7	$873,125	02.1	$566,498	04.25
05	$401,445	10.9	$891,461	15.1	$590,574	04.25
06	$445,202	04.9	$1,026,071	26.5	$615,673	04.25
07	$467,017	15.8	$1,297,980	(37.0)	$641,839	04.25
08	$540,806	05.5	$817,727	05.5	$669,118	04.25
09	$570,550	(37.0)	$862,702	15.8	$697,555	04.25
10	$359,447	26.5	$999,009	04.9	$727,201	04.25
11	$454,700	15.1	$1,047,961	10.9	$758,107	04.25
12	$523,360	02.1	$1,162,189	28.7	$790,327	04.25

The fly in the ointment is withdrawals. People save for retirement so they can begin withdrawing money for income once they retire. Look what happens to our same

---

42 Michael Finke, Wade Pfau & David Blanchett, "The 4% Rule is Not Safe in a Low-Yield World," Journal of Financial Planning 5 Feb 2014.

two portfolios using the same assumptions but adding in withdrawals, in this case a $30,000 annual withdrawal.

	Actual S&P 500			S&P 500 Reversed			Avg Rate of Return		
YEAR	BEGINNING BALANCE	HISTORICAL RETURN %	WITHDRAWAL	BEGINNING BALANCE	RETURN %	WITHDRAWAL	BEGINNING BALANCE	RETURN %	WITHDRAWAL
01	$500,000	(09.1)	$30,000	$500,000	13.7	$30,000	$500,000	04.25	$30,000
02	$424,500	(11.9)	$30,000	$538,500	32.4	$30,000	$491,250	04.25	$30,000
03	$343,985	(22.1)	$30,000	$682,974	16.0	$30,000	$482,128	04.25	$30,000
04	$237,964	28.7	$30,000	$762,250	02.1	$30,000	$472,619	04.25	$30,000
05	$276,260	10.9	$30,000	$748,257	15.1	$30,000	$462,705	04.25	$30,000
06	$276,372	04.9	$30,000	$831,244	26.5	$30,000	$452,370	04.25	$30,000
07	$259,914	15.8	$30,000	$1,021,524	(37.0)	$30,000	$441,596	04.25	$30,000
08	$20,981	05.5	$30,000	$613,560	05.5	$30,000	$430,363	04.25	$30,000
09	$255,884	(37.0)	$30,000	$617,306	15.8	$30,000	$418,654	04.25	$30,000
10	$131,207	26.5	$30,000	$684,840	04.9	$30,000	$406,447	04.25	$30,000
11	$135,977	15.1	$30,000	$688,397	10.9	$30,000	$393,721	04.25	$30,000
12	$126,510	02.1	$30,000	$733,432	28.7	$30,000	$380,454	04.25	$30,000
13	$99,166	16.0	$30,000	$913,927	(22.1)	$30,000	$366,623	04.25	$30,000
14	$85,033	32.4	$30,000	$681,949	(11.9)	$30,000	$352,204	04.25	$30,000
15	$82,584	13.7	$30,000	$570,797	(09.1)	$30,000	$337,173	04.25	$30,000
16	$63,898		$30,000	$488,855		$30,000	$321,503		$30,000

After 15 years, the $500,000 portfolio suffering losses in its first few years has barely enough money to cover two more years of withdrawals, whereas the portfolio avoiding losses in the early years has provided a $30,000 annual income for 15 years and still retains a principal balance of almost the full starting amount.

The problem with theories like the 4% rule, Monte Carlo simulations and other statistical projections is that no one can predict what the markets will do in the future, or what interest rates will be, what level of volatility the markets will experience, what inflation will do or what the sequence of returns will be. That's a lot of variables, any one of which can have an adverse effect on your retirement. But none of them can obliterate an optimistic projection like bad timing.

The following chart presents a dramatic illustration of

the effect of early losses on a retirement portfolio. It depicts two retirement portfolios that started at $250,000. Both plans withdrew 5% annually with an adjustment of 3% per year for inflation. Both plans averaged a respectable 6.6% annual rate of return over a 30-year period. The only difference was "Investor A" suffered three consecutive negative years at the start of his retirement.

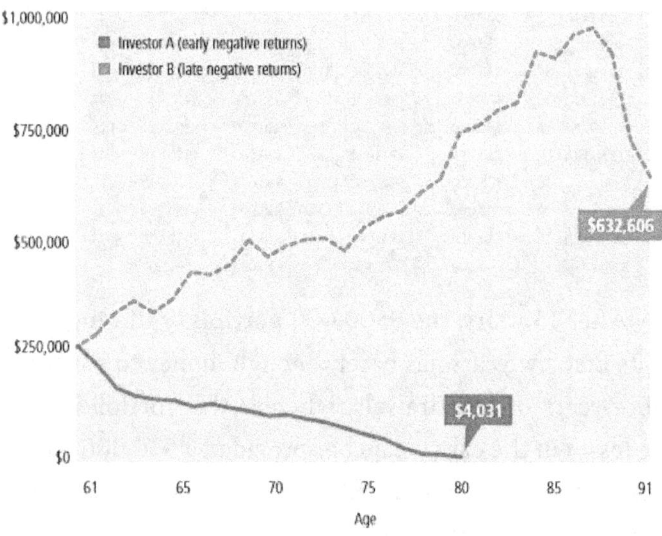

We've never had more resources and done less with them.

Using the S&P 500 returns as a benchmark, someone who retired at the beginning of 1988 experienced just one down year—a tolerable -3.1% in 1990—over the first 11 years of retirement. The cumulative return over that period was 238.21%, a number that would make any retiree giddy! However, someone who retired 12 years later at the beginning of 2000 suffered consecutive losses of 9.1, 11.89 and 22.1% or a cumulative loss of 43.09% of their retirement principal in their first three years. That's the destructive potential of retiring at the wrong time if your primary source of income is tied to the market.

If you leave yourself vulnerable to the sequence of returns, your retirement projections – and your retirement plans—can suffer irreparable damage. You must find a way to offset its potentially destructive impact. I'll discuss some alternatives to help you achieve this goal in a coming chapter.

> *Accept responsibility for your life. Know that it is you who will get you where you want to go, no one else."*

> —LES BROWN

CHAPTER NINE

FINDING INCOME STREAM

"I have always paid income tax. I object only when it reaches a stage when I am threatened with having nothing left for my old age - which is due to start next Tuesday or Wednesday."

—NOEL COWARD

Imagine your area is hit by a hurricane and ensuing flood. You run out of food and there's no sign of rescue. You're forced to risk the rising waters using your only option, an inflatable raft.

I don't like your chances.

The retirement landscape presents a similar challenge. Guaranteed pensions have run out and Social Security may not be there to help you. Your hope of securing an adequate income stream relies on your 401(k), a rubber raft threatened by an increasingly volatile stock market.

I don't like your chances.

The stock market has become an awfully dangerous place. Quoting an article in *Forbes*: *"There are only two ways to beat the stock market in the long-term, net of expenses: one, trade on superior information; two, be lucky. Getting lucky has a much higher probability of working than finding superior information. Finding superior information is very difficult. Most mutual fund managers underperform the market, even with access to a talented pool of analysts. Once in a while they'll get it right, but it's not often enough to make up their cost.*[43]

In his book, *Thinking Fast and Slow*, Princeton professor Daniel Kahneman explains that the human brain is incapable of creating new information—it doesn't know what it doesn't know. To compensate for the unknown, our brains attempt to piece together the best possible story based on what we do know. Sometimes this story is accurate and sometimes not. When we're right, we think it's because we're smart, and when we're wrong, we think it's because we didn't have enough information and there was nothing we could do about it.

We've never been more educated and yet more confused.

Aside from your health, the biggest challenge you will face in retirement is creating a sufficient income stream. With two legs of the retirement stool—pensions and Social Security—effectively gone, how do you replace that income?

If you listen to the financial media and Wall Street brokers, you'll hear them promote portfolio growth. That sounds good but I don't see any growth? If you were invested in an S&P index fund for the past two years, you would be virtually even. It will take some investors years to make up what they lost in the month of January 2016 alone. Some abandoned the equity market in favor of the perceived safety of bonds, CDs and money market funds,

---

43   Rick Ferri, "Why Smart People Fail to Beat the Market," Forbes 21 Mar 2012.

but in the prevailing interest rate environment, that strategy doesn't even keep pace with inflation.

Chasing growth is chasing a rainbow. You need some growth but come retirement, it's time to put growth in the back seat and more aggressively pursue income replacement. You will need multiple income replacement vehicles.

We know what to do but we don't do what we know.

You need consistent, reliable income if you are to maintain the same standard of living in retirement that you enjoyed during your working years. You need to find alternatives for the growth that isn't there. You need income that you can count on for the 20, 30 or more years you will be retired. Where do you find that income?

The new, fragile financial environment requires a blending of assets, including those from outside the traditional investment box. There are a variety of options with the potential to generate a dependable income stream.

You will not only need retirement income, you will need more income than you imagine. It's been my experience that people planning their retirement consistently underestimate the amount of income they will need to maintain their lifestyle and be able to do the things they want.

People expect their expenses to be lower in retirement, but once they stop working, they have much more free time and that time tends to get filled with activities that cost money, including travel and hobbies. Then too, medical expenses tend to increase faster than expected.

People think they will pay less tax in retirement, but while they may be in a lower tax bracket, they will have fewer deductions and so a higher percentage of their income will go to pay taxes. Withdrawals from qualified 401(k) and IRA plans are taxable as well.

People tend to underestimate their healthcare costs or misunderstand what expenses Medicare and supplemental coverage will and won't cover. They may assume if they eventually require nursing home care, Medicare will cover them, but it may not. If it does, it will only cover a certain number of days. The premiums on Medicare and supplemental policies continue to rise as well, sometimes dramatically as has been the case in the years following the passage of Obamacare.

"I thought my knees would be the first thing
to go, but it was my money."

Many investors ignore the disclaimers and base their decisions on the past performance of stocks. They also ignore the historical data that warns them about the volatility of the markets and the potential for losses. A retirement portfolio composed of 60% stocks and 40% Treasuries is considered reasonably conservative by most advisors yet that simple asset mix is subject to significant loss of principal. The following chart illustrates that point. Evaluated over more than 100 years of market history, the 60/40 portfolio is subject to negative real returns 15% of the time for a portfolio held for 10 years; 20% of the time for a portfolio held 5 years; and a staggering 35% risk of loss for portfolios held one year.

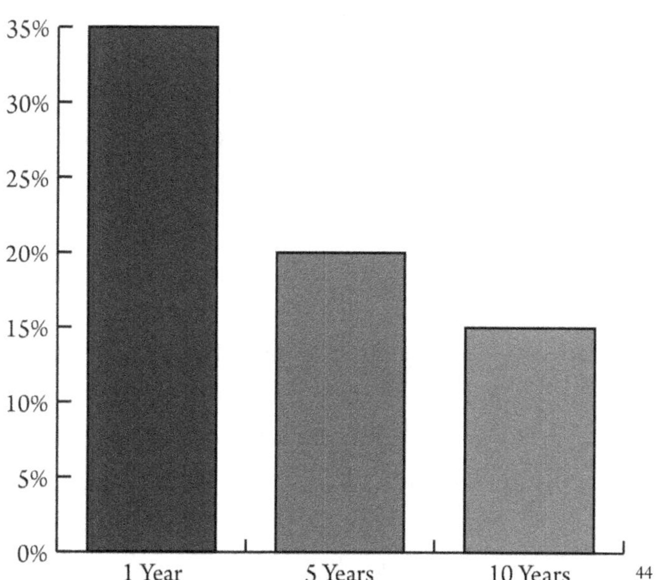

Probability of Negative Real Returns
60/40 U.S. Stock/Treasury Portfolio(1900 - 2012)

People tend to miscalculate the amount of time it takes to recover from a significant market loss. You never make up for losses as quickly as they occurred and a 20% loss in portfolio value requires a 25% gain just to get back even.

44   Source: Shiller, Federal Reserve

When the loss occurs during your retirement, you are also withdrawing money from your portfolio for income. That compounds the problem. If you lose 20% in one year and you also withdraw 5%, you've lost 25% of your investment principal. You must now achieve a 33% gain to get back to ground zero.

> *Rule # 1: Never lose money. Rule # 2: Never forget rule # 1.*
>
> —WARREN BUFFET

The financial meltdown of 2008 exposed much of what was previously hidden from the investing public. Just as when the ocean tide ebbs, everything from bicycle tires to empty beer bottles are uncovered, when the financial tide went out it exposed the cost structures of the banks, insurance and investment companies.

Our economy has always been plagued by boom/bust cycles, some more dramatic than others. What has changed is the increasing velocity of these cycles, making credit crises more common. In recent years, the Fed has attempted to mollify the impact by manipulating the business cycle. However, their repeated attempts to create "soft landings" have only succeeded in putting the Fed into a box from which it may never be able to extricate itself. Simply put, there are no more bullets in their gun.

This should be a warning shot to our generation now approaching an unknown retirement. The country needs more transparency in how its economy is being influenced and controlled by the political class. Whether that ever occurs is doubtful, but as investors, we are not without resources. We need the knowledge, courage and conviction to overcome the effects of an increasingly volatile economic environment. It can be done, but only if you will take personal responsibility for your retirement and explore the available investment alternatives.

CHAPTER TEN

I'M PROUD OF MY WORK

"One of the funny things about the stock market is that every time one person buys, another sells, and both think they are astute."

—WILLIAM FEATHER

A friend called me after a recent market correction to say everyone was telling him to get out of market. I asked, "Who's everybody? Your friends at the club? Your neighbor? The water cooler crowd at work? Who?"

"Well, you know...."

Indeed I do. There are all kinds of external influences—friends, family, coworkers, the media, the Wall Street marketing machinery—that conspire to undermine even the soundest financial plan. I see people make financial decisions based on rumors or advice from friends or media talking heads who don't know any more about what the markets will do next week than they do.

People jump to misguided financial conclusions in minutes but spend three hours clipping grocery coupons to save $20. They spend more time planning their annual vacation than their 30-year retirement. They turn over their investment portfolio to anyone with a good story and a series 6 securities license, an "accreditation" that can be secured over a weekend. It's not unlike trusting your children to a babysitter without checking her background or references.

They give their money to someone who tells them what they want to hear and can't understand what happened when they lose it. So they go island hopping on to the next advisor with a good story and the whole disappointing journey repeats itself. They continuously fall prey to good storytelling instead of learning to understand the process. They continue to lose money and never make up their losses.

We know what to do but we don't do what we know.

SHARKS AND MINNOWS

People selling financial products are no different than people selling automobiles, mattresses, shoes or vacuum cleaners. They have to somehow create action. In the financial industry, fear and greed tend to stimulate action, so that's what they sell. If a prospect says he wants a double-digit return on his money, the broker may sell him a stock or fund that produced double-digit returns—last year. Peddling last year's winners may be a successful sales strategy for some brokers, despite the ubiquitous disclaimers that "past performance is no guarantee of future results."

But that ominous warning does little to dissuade many investors from taking the bait and leaping into funds that were the previous year's best performers. Citing numerous studies, Adam Reed, a finance professor at the University of North Carolina, notes, "Investors have a tendency to rush into funds that are at the top of the previous year's performance rankings."

A report from research and consulting firm Cerulli Associates found that past performance was the most frequently cited factor in choosing funds—by 47% of investors.

A research paper examining a buy-and-hold strategy using a selection of mutual funds that consistently outperformed other funds reports that "Investors are faced with a dilemma; they are told that past performance is no guarantee of future returns, but simultaneously told to choose mutual funds using primarily past performance data. Most analyses of mutual fund past performance are suspect because funds that have been terminated or merged, are not included in the analyses; it is these terminated and merged funds that tend to have the worst performance record."[45]

Consider a hypothetical portfolio that, each January 1, began following the strategy espoused by the investment newsletter that had the best record over the previous year. Over the past two decades, this portfolio would have been a disaster, losing an average 17% a year. The strategy didn't trail the S&P 500 every year, but in the majority of years it did, it suffered huge losses. That's because one-year performance rankings will almost always be dominated by high-risk strategies that hit it big. When they don't pan out, those same strategies also can lose big.[46]

---

45   Babriel Asebedo and John Grable, "Predicting Mutual Fund Over-Performance Over A Nine-Year Period," Association for Financial Counseling and Planning Education 2004.
46   Mark Hulbert, "Why Following the Winners Is for Losers," Wall Street Journal 3 Jan 2014.

I hear stories from people who were sold investments that seemingly made no sense whatsoever, given their circumstances. In my experience, there is rampant incompetence in the financial industry because the bar to enter the business is ridiculously low. When the car business or real estate industry slows down, an avalanche of neophytes floods into the financial advisory industry. I call them weeds in our garden; weeds that need to be pulled. The only way to do it is to raise the bar to get in.

I've seen examples where retirees were sold annuities paying brokers up to 12% commissions, a shameless practice. It's one reason why I acquired the CFP® (CERTIFIED FINANCIAL PLANNER™) designation. The CFP® certification process identifies advisors who have met rigorous professional standards and have agreed to adhere to the principles of integrity, objectivity, competence, fairness, confidentiality, professionalism and diligence when dealing with clients. Securing the certification meant many nights and weekends away from my family but I wanted to be regarded as among the most trustworthy and knowledgeable in the business. I wanted to separate myself from those in the business who are out to make a fast buck peddling products that may cause investors to lose money net after fees, commissions and expenses. They're like roach motels; the money checks in but never checks out.

> " I do not regard a broker as a member of the human race."
>
> —HONORE DE BALZAC

Politicians spout platitudes about cleaning up the

industry but the legislation they do manage to pass invariably makes thing worse, not better, especially for the average investor. Nobody is engaging the process and all the while, it's falling apart. You've no doubt heard comparisons to the fall of Rome, where the more educated the population became, the fatter, happier, lazier and less productive they grew. The decline in our country is happening at a comparable—and equally alarming—rate.

"I finally put something aside for my retirement.
I put aside my plans to retire!"

I believe what is commonly referred to as money management may be little more than money marketing. Computer programs lurk behind the scenes for most money managers. These are advisors who take your money, pass investment management off to a third party and collect a point on the assets. They may not be engaged in managing your money. They may simply collect money, send it on to someone else, tack on a point for themselves and not have to do anything more than wine and dine their clients.

That's great in the years where the market does well and they can ride the wave, but a potential disaster when the market plunges. It's advisory incompetence. They're playing with your future. In the past, if you made a mistake with your personal investment, you still had the other two legs of the retirement stool—guaranteed pension and Social Security—to prop you up. Today's Hidden Generation doesn't have that luxury. We cannot afford to lose our personal savings because that's about all we have left.

I know a woman who lost her husband a few years ago. She sold the commercial real estate the couple owned so she could move closer to her daughter in Arizona. She gave the $800,000 she realized from the property to a broker who invested it using a long-term, buy and hold strategy. My God, the woman was 76 years old! She was not a long-term growth investor; she relied on that money to generate retirement income. By the time I met her at a financial seminar, she was down to $375,000. I asked why she was still with that broker. Amazingly, she responded that, "He's such a nice fellow. He takes me out to lunch and we talk for hours." I said, "He lost 400,000 dollars of your money. That sounds like incompetence to me." It's amazing how people will rationalize their financial decisions, even when they prove to be disastrous. That broker is not a nice guy; he's an incompetent guy who lost more than half that elderly woman's money.

Sad to say, that is not an isolated example. It occurs with gruesome regularity in our industry. Think about this: the person selling retirees investments could be someone who left a job bartending two weeks ago, got his series 6 license and is now selling investments to trusting people who now rely on him to provide their retirement income. What a joke. Shame on our industry for allowing things like this to continue. No wonder financial advisors regularly rate below car salesmen in surveys. We deserve it when someone can evaporate half of a retiree's only source of income and continue doing so by schmoozing her and buying an occasional lunch. Unfortunately, the mathematics of that woman's 50% loss is that it will take 10 years at a 7% annual rate of return just to get her back to even. If she leaves her money with that broker, she may never back to even.

"If you had taken tomorrow's advice
yesterday, you'd be rich today!"

We've never been more educated and yet more confused.

People regularly abdicate responsibility for managing their money to someone else because of laziness, indifference, fear or misplaced trust. Those they delegate to may be no smarter than the investors they are taking it from. They may be less honest. It's not too hard to get into our industry and immediately begin making money offering financial advice. I believe the industry needs more people with a clear vision of how solve the longevity issue and help retirees replace income, not more salespeople.

IT'S UP TO YOU

Change is obviously necessary, but whether the industry will police itself and make the needed corrections is doubtful. Like our nation's porous borers, as long as no one is guarding the entry into the financial industry, the competent, inept and deceitful alike will flood in. It becomes your task to separate the capable from the bungling, the honest from the corrupt.

You can't tell the difference if you don't educate yourself. You must take the time to become aware of the options and alternatives available so you can ask intelligent questions and get straight answers. That way, if you want to continue driving down the road, you at least know where the alternative routes lie. The buck stops with you, not with your advisor. Just as you listen to your doctor but also become educated about your medical options, you better know something more than stocks and bonds and buy and hold if you plan to retire successfully.

Don't let yourself become paralyzed by the seeming complexity of the issues surrounding sound retirement planning. I hear it all the time: "I can't do anything about it right now; I want to wait and see who gets into office; When I have more free time, I'll explore my options..."

If you start to rationalize putting off retirement decisions, you will only fall into a deeper and deeper ennui. You could get away with riding the wind when you had a guaranteed pension and a solvent Social Security system. That's over and done. While the future is unknown, you have to take the reins of your own little wagon. Things aren't going to stop or even slow down. Think how quickly the past ten years flew by; the next ten will pass just as quickly. Retirement sneaks up on you while you are planning to do something about it next year.

We've never had more reasons to succeed and yet wasted more time.

I sometimes think people just grow more numb as the world gets crazier. Our institutions and political class disappoint us. They have their own agenda and it doesn't include taking care of you. The campaign speeches sound promising but nothing happens once they reach office, nothing that will help your retirement in any case. It's easy to believe the best days of our country are behind us. An unhappy result is we become psychologically apathetic. Apathy is the worst environment when you have investments because it becomes a continuum. You can't fall asleep at the wheel and expect to wake up at retirement and everything will somehow have taken care of itself. That may be the message our industry perpetuates but it's not reality.

I've been advising people for a quarter of a century and I consider myself a reasonably intelligent person yet I can't even figure out how a mutual fund can post a return. I have people tell me they are getting a certain return on their funds, but when I ask them how they arrived at that figure, they say it's what their broker told them. Those numbers may be highly inaccurate. The actual annual return on a mutual fund can be determined rather simply by deducting the amount of money in your account on January 1 from the amount in your account on December 31, plus or minus any additions.

Investors may often lack a baseline for measurement. Beyond that, they may not know what their actual return is because they may not understand what they are paying in commissions, fees, expenses and other charges. I sometimes feel as though they are human lemmings, driving down the road, headed for the cliff, and I'm powerless to stop them.

Ask a few people what they made on their money last year. I'll bet not more than one in twenty will know for certain. People rarely know, and if they throw out a figure, it's what their broker told them the fund made. But their fund is a blind pool of investors moving in and out of the fund. That's not their return. When I tell people to call their broker and ask for an accurate accounting of what they made the previous year, I can count on them calling me back in a few days to say their broker couldn't answer the question... beyond repeating the bromide of what the fund made. That's irrelevant but it's all he's got to say because he is not engaged. He's busy selling.

When I conduct quarterly or annual reviews with clients, I tell them what we made during the previous period. They deserve an accurate accounting of what I did with their money, even if it's a loss. If the market corrected 15% and we corrected 2%, I think we managed the risk well. We are engaged. There's no mystery about what's happening or where they are. I try to put myself in the shoes of my client. I would want to know exactly where I am at. I would want to know all my options and plan to make sure I have the income tools that are going to get me to the retirement I want. I want to know with reasonable certainty that I will have the income stream I need to maintain my lifestyle once I retire. I sure as hell don't want to be investing to chase growth.

I call it the pillow test. You have to be able to fall asleep without worrying about your money. If you have so much stress over your finances that you can't sleep, get out of the market.

> " I finally know what distinguishes man from the other beasts: financial worries."
>
> —JULES RENARD

The volatility that has become an inherent characteristic of the market is not going away. If anything, it will only exacerbate. The violent corrections do more psychological than financial harm to investors. The market is a dangerous place. If it's too much for you to handle comfortably, don't be embarrassed. Get out. Find alternatives. If you have been managing your own money, you may find some serenity buy getting professional help. But make sure you are putting your trust in someone who is trustworthy. Don't be lazy and trust your intuition. Do your homework. Check references. Take your time. Make an educated choice. Find an advisory partner who will always put your best interests first, not the other way around. That's critical.

We know what to do but we don't always do what we know.

WHY AM I DOING THIS?

My wife occasionally asks me why I continue to put myself through the angst of worrying about my clients. "We have plenty of money," she says. She is also a successful businessperson, having built and managed thriving advertising agency, so she's not whistling into the wind.

I ask myself why I continue to do it. Am I just a lone wolf wailing at the moon with no one listening? I don't think so. I've been fortunate and successful so I no longer have to do it. I could simply go with the flow like so many others in the industry. Delegate investment management of my clients' assets to a "name" outside firm, shut up, collect my one percent and go play golf.

The fact is, while I don't have to do this, I want to because I believe that the message needs to be heard. Something inside of me says I'm put here for a reason. I want to express that reason. It may not change the world but it can change enough people to make it worthwhile. It's better than knowing these things and doing nothing about it, instead joining the majority and contributing to the financial myth.

There are some prospects I meet that don't become clients because they don't hear what they want to hear from me. Not everyone can handle the truth. But that doesn't matter because my integrity and convictions remain intact. I take care of my deliberately limited little universe of clients.

Your relationship with your financial advisor is likely the second most critical affiliation in your life, superseded only by that with your physician. Money is of little value if you squander your health. My clients know that their world is the most important universe to me.

www.ingramcontent.com/pod-product-compliance
Lightning Source LLC
Chambersburg PA
CBHW050949050726